REVELATIONS

ALSO BY ELAINE PAGELS

Beyond Belief: The Secret Gospel of Thomas

The Origin of Satan

Adam, Eve, and the Serpent: Sex and Politics in Early Christianity

The Gnostic Gospels

Reading Judas: The Gospel of Judas and the Shaping of Christianity
(with Karen King)

Elaine Pagels

REVELATIONS

Visions, Prophecy, and Politics in
the Book of Revelation

VIKING

VIKING
Published by the Penguin Group
Penguin Group (USA) Inc., 375 Hudson Street,
New York, New York 10014, U.S.A.
Penguin Group (Canada), 90 Eglinton Avenue East, Suite 700, Toronto,
Ontario, Canada M4P 2Y3 (a division of Pearson Penguin Canada Inc.)
Penguin Books Ltd, 80 Strand, London WC2R 0RL, England
Penguin Ireland, 25 St. Stephen's Green, Dublin 2, Ireland
(a division of Penguin Books Ltd)
Penguin Books Australia Ltd, 250 Camberwell Road, Camberwell,
Victoria 3124, Australia (a division of Pearson Australia Group Pty Ltd)
Penguin Books India Pvt Ltd, 11 Community Centre,
Panchsheel Park,New Delhi–110 017, India
Penguin Group (NZ), 67 Apollo Drive, Rosedale, Auckland 0632,
New Zealand (a division of Pearson New Zealand Ltd)
Penguin Books (South Africa) (Pty) Ltd, 24 Sturdee Avenue,
Rosebank, Johannesburg 2196, South Africa

Penguin Books Ltd, Registered Offices: 80 Strand, London WC2R 0RL, England

First published in 2012 by Viking Penguin, a member of Penguin Group (USA) Inc.

1 3 5 7 9 10 8 6 4 2

Frontispiece: Albrecht Dürer (1471–1528). Saint Michael fighting the dragon. Woodcut from The Revelation of St. John (Rev. XII, 7–9). 1498 (B.71). Bibliothèque Nationale, Paris. Photo credit: Bridgeman-Giraudon / Art Resources, New York.

LIBRARY OF CONGRESS CATALOGING IN PUBLICATION DATA
Pagels, Elaine H.
Revelations: visions, prophecy, and politics in the Book of Revelation / Elaine Pagels.
p. cm.
Includes bibliographical references and index.
ISBN 978-0-670-02334-9
1. Bible. N.T. Revelation—Criticism, interpretation, etc. 2. Eschatology. I. Title.
BS2825.52.P34 2012
228'.06—dc23   2011037551

Printed in the United States of America
Set in Adobe Jenson Pro
Designed by Francesca Belanger

To James
with love

CONTENTS

CHAPTER ONE

John's Revelation:
Challenging the Evil Empire, Rome

The Book of Revelation is the strangest book in the Bible—and the most controversial.

Instead of stories and moral teaching, it offers only visions— dreams and nightmares. And although few people say they understand its powerful images and prophecies, the book has been wildly popular among readers for two thousand years. Even today, countless people throughout the world turn to it to find meaning, and many Christian groups claim to see its prophecies of divine judgment being fulfilled before their eyes. Millions fear being "left behind" when the end comes, as Tim LaHaye's best-selling book series warns, and believe that they are seeing its prophesied battles playing out in catastrophic events of recent history. Its visions of heaven and hell weave through literature from Milton's *Paradise Lost* to the poems of William Butler Yeats and the stories of James Baldwin, and have inspired music ranging from "Battle Hymn of the Republic" and African American spirituals to the *Quartet for the End of Time*, which French composer Olivier Messiaen wrote and first performed in a Nazi prison camp. Filmmakers and artists today graphically picture its visions, as Michelangelo, Goya, Bosch, Blake, and Picasso did before them. Christians in America have identified with its visions of cosmic war since the 1600s, when many immigrating to the New World believed they had arrived in the "new Jerusalem" promised in Revelation. Many have seen America as a "redeemer nation" that is to bring in the millennium, while others see its present military and economic system as evil Babylon.[1] Political rhetoric still appeals to our nation's sense of divine destiny—or damns America for its sins.

How did this book speak to people when it was written two thousand years ago, and how does it continue to do so today? These questions led to this book, for, whether we love or hate it, the Book of Revelation speaks to something deep in human nature. I began this writing during a time of war, when some who advocated war claimed to find its meaning in Revelation, which was itself written in the aftermath of war. Exploring how this book has fascinated readers for two thousand years tells us much about ourselves and about how religion evokes such powerful responses—for better and for worse—to this day.

Controversy about the Book of Revelation is nothing new: Ever since it was written, Christians have argued heatedly for and against it, especially from the second century to the fourth, when it barely squeezed into the canon to become the final book in the New Testament.[2] When critics charged that a heretic had written it, its earliest defenders sought to lend it legitimacy by insisting that Jesus' own disciple John wrote its prophecies, in addition to the Gospel of John. Around the year 260, however, the famous Egyptian bishop called Saint Dionysius of Alexandria challenged their view, pointing out that the style of the two books differs markedly and arguing that the sophisticated gospel writer could not have written such clumsy Greek.[3] Dionysius added that "I have not said these things to pour scorn upon [the author of Revelation]—do not imagine that!—but only to show how different the two books are," for he agreed that Revelation had been written "by a holy and inspired writer."[4] Nevertheless, debates about its authenticity—and its place in the New Testament—persisted. More than a thousand years later, Martin Luther wanted to throw the Book of Revelation out of the canon, saying "there is no Christ in it," until he realized how he could use its powerful imagery against the Catholic Church, while Catholic apologists turned it back against him and other "protesting" Christians.[5] Many Christians never speak about it; some refuse to read it in worship; others talk about it all the time. The story of the Book of Revelation and how Christians have read it takes us from the time when Jesus' followers were a marginal and persecuted minority to the emergence of a flourishing movement and then the establishment of the New Testament canon, after the emperor Constantine suddenly took Christ as his patron and made Christianity the dominant religion of the Roman Empire.

Who wrote this book? Why—and how—do so many people still read it today? And what *is* revelation? Are any so-called revelations what they claim to be: messages from God? How can we know whether these visions actually communicate truth about reality or only one person's projection or delusion? Asking such questions, I realized that what complicates our story is the long-hidden cache of ancient Christian writings discovered in Egypt in 1945—a discovery that includes not only the so-called Gnostic gospels but also about twenty *other* "books of revelation"—most of them quite different from the New Testament Book of Revelation.[6] Many of them speak less about a Judgment Day at the end of the world than about finding the divine in it now. But before we explore these, let's look at what we find in the New Testament Book of Revelation.

This book opens as its author, John (often called John of Patmos, since he says he wrote it on the small island of Patmos, off the coast of Turkey), tells how he was "in the spirit"[7]—in an ecstatic trance—one Sunday when suddenly he heard a loud voice speaking to him. Turning, John says he saw a divine being announce "what is going to happen soon" to bring on the end of time. John, a Jewish follower of Jesus of Nazareth, believed that this divine being who spoke to him was Jesus, alive after his death, now appearing not in ordinary human form but as a glorious and terrifying presence whose "face was like the sun shining with full force."[8] John says that Jesus announced that God is about to make war on the evil powers that have taken over the world and that, although the coming cosmic war will destroy the entire universe, ultimately God will prevail, throw evildoers into a lake of eternal fire, and welcome the righteous into his kingdom.

John says that he heard a voice telling him to "come up here!"— apparently a summons to ascend into heaven through a door he saw standing open before him.[9] John says that "at once I was in the spirit," allowed to glimpse the throne of God in heaven, looking much as the prophet Ezekiel, writing six hundred years earlier, said he had seen it: blazing with fire as flashes of lightning and peals of thunder burst around it; brilliantly gleaming like emeralds, rainbows, sapphires; glorious light flowing into a sea of glittering crystal. As if in a dream, John sees standing next to God's throne a slaughtered lamb, who offers to show him "what must take place after this."[10] As angels sound trumpets, the Four Horsemen of the Apocalypse burst forth, the first riding on a white horse and wielding a sword; the second, on a fiery red horse, receives a huge sword "so that people would slaughter one another";[11] the third, on a black horse, presages famine; the fourth, on a pale horse, brings death by sword, plague, and wild animals. But before the action begins, John says, he sees standing under the altar "the souls of those who had been slaughtered for their witness to God" crying out in a loud voice: "'Sovereign Lord, holy and true, *how long before you judge and avenge our blood on the inhabitants of the earth?*'"[12]

John then sees four angels standing at the four corners of the earth and placing seals on the foreheads of 144,000 men, the elite troops among God's people—twelve thousand from each of Israel's tribes—to protect them from "the great day of the wrath of God." Suddenly the scene returns to the heavenly throne, where John sees a star fall from heaven, a being who "opens the shaft of the bottomless pit,"[13] from which giant locusts with human faces, women's hair streaming behind them, emerge as an army of monsters led by Abaddon, angel of the abyss.[14]

In heaven, two signs now appear in the sky: a woman "clothed with the sun,"[15] hugely pregnant, writhes and cries out in labor, about to give birth to a male child—God's messiah—while a bright red dragon with seven heads paces in front of her, waiting to devour the infant the moment it is born. The woman escapes, her child is caught up into heaven, and John is shocked to see war break out in heaven.[16] The archangel Michael and his angels are fighting the dragon and his angels, who fight back but are beaten down, get thrown out of heaven, and fall to earth. The frustrated dragon, violently enraged, storms off to make war on the woman and upon all of her children who remain on the earth.

John now sees that the dragon has called forth two huge, hideous beasts as his allies. The first, with seven heads and ten horns, rises out of the sea and receives power to "make war . . . on those who keep the commandments of God and the testimony of Jesus"[17] and to dominate the whole world. His ally, the second beast, who has a mysterious name—a human name, John says, indicated by the number 666—"makes the earth and its inhabitants worship the first beast, and cause all those who would not worship the image of the beast to be killed."[18]

As cosmic war intensifies, John sees seven angels standing in heaven and watches as each, in turn, pours out upon the earth a golden bowl filled with God's wrath. The horror intensifies as the sixth angel pours his bowl on the river Euphrates, near Babylon— and the "spirits of demons" summon all the leaders of the nations "to gather them for battle on the great day of God Almighty,"[19] preparing for the terrible battle at Armageddon, the plain at the foot of Mount Carmel in present-day Israel. As the seventh angel pours his bowl into the air, thundering bursts of lightning precede the most violent earthquake the world has ever known, and the city of Babylon falls, its people cursing God as they die in agony. Now John sees a vision of Babylon as the prophet Isaiah had pictured Israel's ancient enemy Tyre—in the form of a great whore, brilliantly dressed, adorned with jewels, sitting on a scarlet beast with seven heads, drinking the blood of God's people from a golden cup.[20]

When the battle reaches its climax, Jesus appears as a divine warrior, mounted on a white horse as he rides forth from heaven to lead armies of angels into war:

From his mouth comes a sharp sword with which to strike down the nations, and he will rule them with a rod of iron; he will tread the winepress of the fury of the wrath of God

Almighty . . . [and his name is] "King of kings, and Lord of lords."[21]

An angel shouts, announcing that God invites all vultures to come after the battle to a hideous feast, to "eat the flesh of kings, the flesh of captains, the flesh of the mighty, the flesh of the horses and their riders—flesh of all, both free and slave, small and great."[22] The forces join in battle and Satan is thrown into a pit, the dragon chained, the beasts thrown into a lake of fire—while all human beings who had died faithful to God come back to life and reign over the earth for a thousand years. Then Jesus judges the whole world, and all who have worshipped other gods or committed murder, magic, or illicit sexual acts are thrown down to be tormented forever in a lake of fire,[23] while God's faithful are invited to enter a new city of Jerusalem that descends from heaven and where Christ and his people reign in triumph for a thousand years.

Anyone hearing these prophecies might well wonder: What kinds of visions are these, and what kind of man was writing them? John was a Jewish prophet writing visions he claimed to have received on the island of Patmos, about seventy miles from the city of Ephesus, off the coast of Asia Minor in present-day Turkey; but we begin to understand what he wrote only when we see that his book is *wartime literature*. John probably began to write around 90 C.E., having likely fled from a war that had ravaged Judea, his homeland.[24] John may actually have witnessed the outbreak of war in Jerusalem in 66 C.E., when militant Jews, fired with religious fervor, sporadically attacked groups of Roman soldiers and stockpiled weapons to fight an all-out war against Rome's occupation of Judea in the name of "God and our common liberty."

After four years of desperate fighting, Rome sent sixty thousand troops to besiege Jerusalem, starve its inhabitants, and break the revolutionaries' ferocious resistance. When Roman soldiers, led first by the future emperor Vespasian and later by his son Titus, finally defeated the Jews, they desecrated the sacred precincts of the Great Temple, burned it to the ground, and left the inner city of Jerusalem in ruins.[25]

Twenty years later, the prophet John was living on Patmos, where tradition says he was forcibly sent "because of the word of God and the testimony of Jesus Christ."[26] We might imagine him pacing restlessly along the sea by day and lying awake at night, watching the constellations as they moved across the sky.[27] Horrified by the slaughter of so many of his people by Rome, John put his own cry of anguish into the mouths of the souls he says he saw in heaven, pleading for God's justice.

Other Jews among his contemporaries asked similar questions, but John was not a traditional Jew, since he had joined the radical sect devoted to Jesus of Nazareth. Although later Christian tradition identified him as John of Zebedee, one of Jesus' disciples, John of Patmos belonged to the second generation of Jesus' followers, who had heard what the early disciples reported Jesus secretly telling them: that he himself was God's messiah, the chosen future king of Israel.[28] Many first-generation followers of Jesus had expected him to lead Israel to victory over the hated Romans and reestablish God's kingdom in Jerusalem and eventually over the whole world. When Jesus was arrested after one of his inner circle denounced him to the leaders who presided over the Jerusalem Temple, he was brought to Pilate, the Roman governor, who ordered him beaten and crucified as the self-professed "king of the

Jews." After that, many of his followers quit the movement, and Roman magistrates killed its outspoken leaders. Although John apparently was born some years after these events, he probably knew that the Romans had also crucified Peter, Jesus' right-hand man, and had whipped and beheaded Paul of Tarsus. He may have heard various accounts of the violent death of Jesus' own brother James, whom many regarded as his successor, beaten or stoned to death near the Jerusalem Temple.

But some of Jesus' followers—and *their* followers—refused to give up. John, persuaded by their preaching, was one of those in the next generation who insisted that Jesus was still God's appointed future king of Israel—and, indeed, of the whole world. They claimed that God had brought him back to life and that soon Jesus would return from heaven to earth and vanquish his enemies as God's chosen ruler of the universe—"King of kings, and Lord of lords."[29] Jews among John's contemporaries thought Jesus' followers were fools, of course, since Jesus had been killed sixty years before. But had someone asked his loyal followers how they could possibly believe that Jesus would return as king, John could answer that he had seen proof that the most astonishing of Jesus' prophecies had already come true—and so he dared hope that the rest would do the same. For when Jesus announced that "the kingdom of God is coming soon," he also privately warned his followers that before God's kingdom would come, terrible sufferings must first take place—earthquakes, famine, and war, followed by the unthinkable: that enemy armies would surround and besiege Jerusalem and utterly destroy the Great Temple, the sacred center of Jerusalem. The Gospel of Mark says that when Jesus walked through that temple with his disciples, who were awed by its magnificence, he said to them, "Do you see these great buildings? Not one stone will be left here upon another; all will be thrown down."[30] Many historians have suggested that Jesus did not actually prophesy the temple's destruction and that his followers added this saying only after it happened; but I find it more plausible that he did speak this prophecy, as, in any case, many of his followers surely believed.[31] Jesus repeatedly warned that Judgment Day—and God's kingdom—would come within one generation: *"There are some standing here who will not die until they see the kingdom of God having come with power. . . . I tell you, this generation will not pass away until all these things have taken place."*[32]

Imagine how John felt, then, when, about forty years after Jesus' death, this shocking prophecy turned out to be true: in 70 C.E., Roman armies stormed Jerusalem, burned down the temple, and reduced the city center to charred rubble. When this happened, John and others loyal to Jesus were both horrified and excited, for this must mean that everything else he had prophesied would now happen. Jesus had warned that "wars and rumor of wars" would be "only the beginning of the birth pangs [of the messiah]" and told them to expect persecution, saying that "in those days there will be such suffering as has not been from the beginning of the creation until now, no, and never will be."[33] But Jesus had added that, *after* these catastrophic events, his followers would see "the son of man coming in the clouds, with great power and glory," to establish God's kingdom:

> When you see these things taking place, you know that he is near, at the very gates. Truly I tell you, this generation will not pass away before all these things have taken place.[34]

About ten years after the end of the Jewish war, racing against time, some of his followers wrote the gospels of Mark, Matthew, and Luke to spread Jesus' message and warn the rest of the world before the end would come.

Although John may have fled from Judea to Asia Minor, he, like many among the second generation of believers, waited for Jesus to return and for his kingdom to "come with power." But by the time John began to write his Revelation, nearly thirty more years had passed. Now *two* generations had come and gone—and John, along with Jesus' other followers, must have wondered how the prophecy had failed. For when John traveled through Asia Minor, he could see evidence everywhere that the kingdom that actually had "come with power" was not God's—it was *Rome's*.

At the great Asian port of Ephesus, John could have seen the temples, the theaters, the monumental municipal buildings, crowded with statues of pagan gods, and the central street dominated by a colossal statue of Titus, commander of the Roman forces that had burned the Jerusalem Temple. Everywhere he looked, John would have found inscriptions, statues, and temples depicting the triumphs of the Roman gods. The greatest of these was built by Titus' brother, Domitian, the current emperor, who ruled what Romans called "the whole world," from Britain to what is now France, Germany, Spain, and Italy, extending to Croatia and Serbia, Turkey and Greece, and then to Egypt, Africa, Syria, Israel, and as far east as Iraq. Near Ephesus, in the city of Pergamum, John would have seen what he called "Satan's throne" but what local citizens regarded as the pride of their city—the great temple of Zeus, which stood at the top of the city, near the first temple that wealthy city leaders had built to demonstrate their patriotism, and had dedicated to the divine emperor Augustus and to the goddess Roma.[35] And in the nearby city of Aphrodisias, John might have marveled at the huge and lavish temple, three stories high, called the Sebasteion, "temple of the holy ones."[36]

Most travelers who walked through these grand colonnades would have admired the great panels of sculptured reliefs that celebrated Roman victories over nations under imperial rule.[37] John, however, coming from the subject nation of Judea, would have been disgusted by what he saw. Many of the panels picture an armed, godlike emperor dominating a female slave—a metaphor for how Romans saw the nations they conquered. The south portico, for example, commemorates Rome's conquest of Britain, picturing the emperor Claudius seizing an anguished female slave by the hair and raising his sword to cut her throat. The inscription tells that the slave is Britain, shamed and beaten, her breast exposed as she raises her hand in a futile attempt to ward off the death blow. A second scene depicts Nero forcing a naked female slave—in this case Armenia—to the ground. A third scene pictures the triumphant Augustus being honored among the gods by Venus, whom the Greeks called Aphrodite and whom the emperor saw as patron goddess of his predecessor, Julius Caesar. The local citizens revered her as the divine protector of the city they named for her, Aphrodisias.

What might have angered this provincial Jewish prophet even more than the degrading picture of captive nations like his own would be to see Roman triumphs displayed not simply as imperial propaganda but as *religious devotion*. John would have seen such monumental architecture as a demonic parody of God's truth, picturing rulers like Augustus, Nero, and Tiberius, under whose reign Jesus was crucified, as divinely ordained—by gods whom John loathed as demonic powers.

Historians have often assumed that reverence for emperors as gods or heroes was a matter of political expedience, not piety. But Oxford historian Simon Price has brilliantly shown that the matter looked very different to the Asian citizens who built the Sebasteion.[38] The distinction between *religion* and *politics* would have made no sense to them—or, for that matter, to most of their contemporaries. Revering the ruler was less a matter of worshipping a human being than of showing respect for the gods who had placed him there, and so shaped the destiny of nations. The citizens of Asia Minor who commissioned the Sebasteion and funded the annual festivals, sacrifices, and athletic games to honor the emperors chose to interpret their submission to Roman rule not as defeat but as *submission to the will of the gods*. Offering such honors to the Roman emperor and his gods could not only ingratiate them to their rulers but could also ease the harsh reality of subjugation to Rome, and lend it meaning.

The historian Steven Friesen has shown that a political crisis, ignited by Julius Caesar's assassination in 44 B.C.E., impelled leading citizens in the Roman province of Asia to fund the lavish outpouring of imperial temples that John saw in their cities— construction they hoped would win favor with Caesar's successor. For after the emperor's own senators stabbed him to death in the Senate chamber, his death plunged Rome into a leadership crisis. As three rivals fought to succeed him, leading citizens in the province of Asia backed Mark Antony and Cleopatra. Within a few years, however, the Asian leaders discovered that they had sided with the losers. With Antony's defeat, members of Asia's ruling councils quickly sought to placate the winner, Octavian, later called Augustus, by funding in his honor extravagant temples, statues, and religious festivals to demonstrate their newfound loyalty to him—and to Rome and its gods.

Although the story of Antony and Cleopatra often sounds like melodrama, the consequences of their failed war against Octavian helps account for the imperial display that John of Patmos probably encountered in Asia Minor. After Caesar's assassination, his designated heir, the brilliant, rich, and ruthless eighteen-year-old Octavian, took his place. At first Octavian agreed to rule jointly with Mark Antony and Marcus Lepidus, both experienced senior consuls. But when tensions erupted among them, Octavian broke off the alliance, took command of Lepidus' army, and forced him into lifetime exile. Antony, sensing danger, resolved to seize control of the empire before Octavian could take it from him.

To gather support in the Senate, Antony retreated to the eastern provinces of the empire—to Egypt, where he met Cleopatra, whom he had seen on a previous trip about ten years earlier, when she was fourteen and already precocious, fiercely intelligent, and stunningly attractive. Now she presided as queen, and, although formally married to her younger brother, she had previously been the lover of Julius Caesar, to whom she bore a son. After meeting Antony, she allied herself with him and became his consort—and, as his biographer Plutarch later wrote, the love of his life.[39]

In 32 B.C.E., while still married to Octavian's older sister, Octavia, Antony lived openly with Cleopatra in Ephesus as they courted allies to fight his brother-in law. Plutarch tells how shouting, enthusiastic crowds hailed Antony as the living embodiment of the god Dionysus and cheered Cleopatra, who often dressed as the New Isis, in honor of her patron goddess. The two held court for several years. Cleopatra bore him two children while they gained the support of many Asian leaders, including the king of Parthia and the king of Judea, and even three hundred Roman senators who traveled to Ephesus to pledge support against Octavian.

Octavian, meanwhile, ordered his sister to leave the house she had shared with Antony and divorce him. When she refused, pleading with him to not declare war on her husband, Octavian ironically complied by ordering the Senate to declare war on Cleopatra. When war came, Octavian destroyed Antony's navy of five hundred warships at Actium and routed his hundred thousand soldiers and twelve thousand cavalry. Antony was shocked to see hundreds of his ships on fire, and even more horrified to see Cleopatra's navy suddenly turn and join Octavian's fleet. After escaping to a fort where Cleopatra was hiding with a few of her slaves, Antony chose suicide rather than allow Octavian to capture, torture, and kill him. To Octavian's dismay, Cleopatra, too, eluded his grasp, having poisoned herself rather than be brought back to Rome in chains as a trophy in his triumphal parade.

Octavian's victory caused an enormous crisis for Antony's allies, who now had to deal with their enemy as their ruler, one who had mercilessly killed those who opposed him in Rome. When the Roman Senate voted him the honorific title Augustus ("revered one" or "majestic one"), the Asian leaders who had sworn loyalty to Mark Antony now demonstrated their loyalty by offering the new emperor unprecedented honors. Shortly after his victory, the provincial council of Asia humbly petitioned him for permission to honor him as the "divine" Augustus, along with the goddess Roma, and to build a magnificent temple in Pergamum dedicated to the imperial family and to its gods—the first of its kind in Asia. During the decades of the first century C.E., leading citizens of other Asian cities would devote huge amounts of city taxes to vie with one another for the honor—and the advantages— of crowding their cities with statues, arches, and colossal statues dedicated to Rome, its rulers, and its gods.

When John arrived in Ephesus around 90 C.E., apparently having spent some time traveling and preaching in Asia Minor, he might have seen a small army of expert stoneworkers constructing the colossal statues, each about a hundred feet high, of emperor Vespasian and his sons, Titus and Domitian, and building the most spectacular temple in the entire city to honor as *divi* ("divine") the very rulers who had devastated Jerusalem and destroyed the Great Temple of God. Longing for vengeance, John recalled Israel's sacred scriptures: hadn't King David himself declared that "the gods of the nations are demons"?[40] And hadn't the prophets—most recently, Jesus—announced that God would soon come to judge the world? Why would God allow these demonic forces and their arrogant human agents to overrun the world with apparent impunity?

What John did in the Book of Revelation, among other things, was create *anti-Roman propaganda* that drew its imagery from Israel's prophetic traditions—above all, the writings of Isaiah, Jeremiah, Ezekiel, and Daniel. To understand what he was doing, let's take a closer look at what he wrote. We don't know what brought John to the island of Patmos, near Ephesus, but he claims that while he was there, visions came to him—perhaps induced by prayer and fasting[41]—when "I heard behind me a loud voice, like a trumpet," saying, "what you see, write in a book." John says that when he turned to see who was speaking to him, he saw Jesus in the form that the prophet Daniel claimed to have seen the Son of Man more than two hundred years earlier—his hair "white as snow, like white wool," his eyes blazing like flames, face "shining like the sun in full strength. When I saw him," John wrote, "I fell at his feet as though dead."[42] Next, John hears Jesus declare that God's kingdom is, indeed, coming soon—and promise those who endure that "I will keep you from the hour of trial that is coming upon the whole world."[43]

John tells how moments later, having ascended "in the spirit" into the heavens, he was allowed to glimpse the glorious throne of God, the One on the throne radiating light, set among seven flaming torches, much as John had read in Ezekiel's prophecy:

> . . . there was something like a throne, in appearance like sapphire; and seated above the likeness of a throne was something that looked like a human form. Above what looked like the loins, I saw something like gleaming amber, something that looked like fire . . . like the rainbow in a cloud on a rainy day, such was the . . . splendor all around.[44]

Hearing peals of thunder, John sees lightning flash from the throne, surrounded by worshippers and thousands of angels and flanked by four unearthly creatures studded with multiple eyes, one with a lion's face, the others with the faces of a bull, an eagle, and a man. John adds:

> I saw in the right hand of the one seated on the throne a
> scroll . . . sealed with seven seals, and I saw a mighty angel
> proclaiming with a loud voice, "Who is worthy to open the
> scroll and break its seals?"[45]

This sacred scroll reveals God's divine plan—"what must take place after this." Hearing that "no one in heaven, or on earth, or under the earth, was able to open the scroll, or look into it," John says, "I began to weep bitterly." But one of God's servants reassures him: "Do not weep. Behold, the lion of the tribe of Judah, the root of David, has conquered, so that he can open the scroll and its seven seals."[46]

Taking heart, John expects to see the conquering messiah, the king called the Lion of Judah, standing before God's throne, and is astounded to see instead a *lamb*—and, stranger still, "a lamb standing as if it had been slaughtered, having seven horns and seven eyes, which are the seven spirits of God." To his surprise, this supernatural creature takes the scroll and a divine voice pronounces him worthy to open it, "because you were slaughtered, and ransomed God's holy ones from every tribe, language, people, and nation." Thus John hears that this strange figure epitomizes the paradox embodied in Jesus of Nazareth,[47] whose closest followers had recognized—and publicly acclaimed—him as God's appointed king, their messiah. But instead of riding triumphant into Jerusalem for his coronation, as they had hoped, Jesus was slaughtered on the eve of Passover, like a sacrificial lamb.[48] "Then," says John,

> I saw the lamb open one of the seven seals, and I heard one
> of the four living creatures call out, with a voice of thunder,

"Come!" I looked, and there was a white horse! Its rider had a bow; a crown was given to him, and he came out conquering, and to conquer.[49]

Now John begins to see heavenly secrets unfold to show the coming end of time. What he sees next—the Four Horsemen of the Apocalypse—reveals events that have already begun to play themselves out on earth. As we noted, the first horseman signifies war, perhaps indicating the wars that had shattered the empire for decades, reaching new intensity in the year 68 c.e., when four emperors, in turn, were crowned and assassinated.[50] The second horseman, mounted on a bright red horse, "was permitted to take peace from the earth, so that people would slaughter one another." Hearing that the third horseman carries tokens that signify hugely inflated prices for bread and cooking oil, John's contemporaries might recognize that inflation, too, was escalating throughout the empire. Finally John sees a fourth horseman, Death, mounted on a pale green horse, bringing death by plague, famine, and wild animals. Horrifying signs follow: "the sun became black as sackcloth, the full moon became like blood, and the stars of the sky fell to earth, as the fig tree drops its fruits when shaken by a storm," until "the rulers of the earth, and the great men, the generals, the rich and the powerful, and everyone, slaves and free," hide in caves, seeking shelter among rocks on the mountains, "for the great day of [God's] wrath has come, and who is able to stand?"[51]

Yet John sees that *some* will be able to stand, since God sends four angels to protect the sea, earth, and trees and then to protect certain people. An angel explains to John that "we have marked the slaves of God with a seal on their foreheads," first 144,000 men—twelve thousand from each of the twelve tribes of Israel—and, following them, a "great multitude, that no one could count, from every nation, from all tribes and peoples and languages," shouting and singing praise to God. These people, who "have come out of the great ordeal . . . [and] have washed their robes and made them white in the blood of the lamb," now stand before God's throne, waiting to enter Paradise, where Jesus "will guide them to springs of the water of life, and God will wipe away every tear from their eyes."[52]

John now begins to understand why God has delayed the coming judgment: because the end-time events have begun, God wants to protect his "holy ones" from harm. Only after angels seal his people, then, is the lamb allowed to open the seventh seal of the scroll to reveal—and, apparently, to initiate—"what must take place after this." After a suspenseful silence in heaven, John sees seven angels, each sounding a trumpet to signal a series of coming catastrophes:[53] "When the first angel blew his trumpet, hail and fire, mixed with blood" rained down upon the earth, setting a third of the earth on fire. At the second trumpet blast, John says, "something like a great mountain, burning with fire, was thrown into the sea," polluting it so that "a third of the living creatures in the sea died, and a third of the ships were destroyed."[54]

Here John may have had in mind what had happened about ten years before, on August 23 of the year 79 c.e., when Mount Vesuvius, in southern Italy, erupted with a great explosion that shook the earth and filled the air with a deafening roar. As dense clouds of black smoke rose and sheets of flame shot up from the crater, molten lava rained down, killing thousands of people as they fled in terror—burned to death or choked by smoke and falling ashes. Some who watched from afar said that smoke and ashes darkened the sky for more than three days and could be seen as far away as Rome, borne by the wind to Africa, Egypt, and Syria. On the morning of August 27, as the sky began to lighten, what survivors saw was an enormous field of ashes, the cities of Herculaneum and Pompeii completely buried, along with thousands of corpses, animal and human. Witnesses said that the mountain still smoked, and seismic aftershocks shook the earth again and again. Not far from Pompeii lay the famous cave of the Sibyl of Cumae, which, soon afterward, issued an oracle that circulated throughout the Roman world. In the language of oracular tradition, the Sibyl warned that God was about to unleash his wrath on the world, causing earthquakes and raining fire and ashes from the sky—probably referring to Vesuvius. Like John, the oracle's anonymous author recognized these shocking events as signs of the coming end.

While John watched, he says, he heard the fifth angel blow his trumpet and saw a bottomless pit from which smoke arose "like the smoke of a great furnace" and from which a huge army of locusts emerged. Although as big as cavalry horses, these locusts have human faces, hair streaming behind them, teeth like lions, and scorpion tails that sting like serpents, leaving their enemies in hideous pain. Then the scene changes: John says that he saw

> another mighty angel coming down from heaven wrapped in a cloud, with a rainbow over his head; his face was like the sun, and his legs like pillars of fire . . . Setting his right foot on the sea and his left foot on the land, he gave a great shout, like a lion roaring. And when he shouted, the seven

thunders sounded . . . Then the angel raised his right hand
to heaven, and swore by him who lives forever and ever . . .
"There shall be no more time."[55]

When the seventh angel sounds his trumpet, John hears a divine
voice proclaim that God and Jesus have won the victory: "the
kingdom of the world has become the kingdom of our Lord, and
of his anointed one [messiah], and He shall reign forever and
ever."[56] But instead of signaling the end of war, as John expects,
this trumpet call intensifies the conflict. After lightning flashes,
thunder, earthquake, and hail, he sees two great signs appear in the
heavens; first,

> a woman, clothed with the sun, with the moon under her
> feet, and on her head a crown of twelve stars. She was preg-
> nant and was crying out in birth pangs, in the agony of giving
> birth.
>
> Then another sign appeared in heaven: a great red
> dragon, with seven heads and ten horns, and seven crowns
> on his heads. . . . Then the dragon stood before the woman
> who was giving birth, in order to devour her child as soon
> as it was born.[57]

As we noted, now John sees something virtually unprecedented—
war *in heaven*: Michael and his angels fighting the dragon.[58] The
dragon and his angels fight back but are defeated, so that

> there was no longer any place for them in heaven; the great
> dragon was thrown down, that ancient serpent, who is

called the Devil and Satan, the deceiver of the whole world—
he was thrown down to earth, and his angels have been
thrown down with him.[59]

Horrified and fascinated, John watches to see how this heavenly
battle will play out on earth. Furious at having been thrown out of
heaven, the dragon determines to destroy the woman. He pursues
her. She escapes, having been given the wings of a great eagle, and
flies into the wilderness to hide. When the dragon discovers her,
he pours water from his mouth to sweep her away in a thundering
flood, but she eludes him again as "the earth came to the help of
the woman" and swallowed the threatening waters. Raging with
frustration, "the dragon was angry with the woman, and went off
to make war on the rest of her children."

Now the dragon stands on the seashore and calls forth two
monsters as allies:

> And I saw a beast rising out of the sea, having ten horns
> and seven heads; and on its horns were ten crowns, and on
> its heads were blasphemous names. And the beast that I
> saw was like a leopard, its feet were like a bear's, and its
> mouth was like a lion's mouth. And the dragon gave it his
> power and his throne and great authority . . . In amaze-
> ment *the whole earth . . . worshipped the dragon, for he had
> given his authority to the beast, and they worshipped the beast,
> saying, "Who is like the beast; who can fight against it?"*[60]

Arrogant, huge, spewing out blasphemies, the beast from the sea
"was given authority over every tribe and people and language and

nation, and all the inhabitants of the earth will worship it." A second monster emerges from the land, a beast with power to force everyone on earth "to be marked on the right hand or the forehead" with "the mark, that is, the *name* of the beast"—apparently a number with secret meaning, "for it is the number of a human being: his number is six hundred sixty-six." Only the children of the woman whom John saw in his vision dare resist—and for this the beast is determined to kill them.

What could these nightmare visions mean? And where is Rome—and the aftermath of war—to be seen in them? A close reader of the Hebrew Scriptures would see that John was invoking prophetic images to interpret the conflicts of his own time, just as the prophets Isaiah and Jeremiah had interpreted the Babylonian War around six hundred years earlier. These ancient prophets had drawn upon what is perhaps the oldest story in the Bible, one that can be traced to ancient Babylonia, where priests inscribed it in cuneiform on clay tablets more than 2,500 years ago—a story probably told for hundreds, perhaps even thousands, of years before that. The story tells how, "in the beginning," or even *before* the beginning of time, God fought against a great sea monster, the dragon of chaos, to bring forth the world. The Babylonian version tells how the sun god Marduk fought his mother, the great female dragon Tiamat, and her army of monsters, who embodied the ocean depths, the dangerous power of chaos. When Tiamat opened her huge jaws to devour him, Marduk drove the four winds into her mouth, distending her body, then split her in two "like a shrimp" to create from her the earth and sky, and placed them under his own dominion.[61]

Nearly three thousand years ago, Israel's poets and storytellers, familiar with such ancient stories, began to tell how Israel's God, like Marduk, fought against a many-headed dragon, a sea monster whom they called by such names as Leviathan and Rahab. Some said that only after crushing and killing such monsters could God, like Marduk, establish the world and deliver it from the powers of chaos. Thus the author of Psalm 74 praises God for having vanquished Leviathan:

> God, my king, is from old, working salvation in the earth. You divided the sea by your might; you broke the heads of the dragons in the waters; you crushed the heads of Leviathan; you gave him as food for the creatures of the wilderness.[62]

John's visions of such monsters, then, are modeled on creation stories even older than those in Genesis. Many scholars have pointed out that the opening chapters of Genesis were written considerably later than many other biblical writings—probably about *four hundred years* later than the chapters that follow—and later than some of the psalms.[63] Yet whoever wrote the opening of Genesis probably *knew* the ancient dragon story, for Genesis says that even before God created the world, he began not with *nothing,* as Jewish and Christian theologians and philosophers later claimed, but with a formless void, chaos, wind, and "deep waters":

> In the beginning, when God created the heavens and the earth, the earth was *a formless void [or chaos] and darkness covered the surface of the deep waters,* while a wind from God swept over the waters.[64]

Some people thought that this ancient story implied that God's power is limited, since it suggests that God, like Marduk, had to contend with a supernatural antagonist *before* he could create the world. Israel's storytellers, perhaps to reassure their hearers that God's power is uncontested, morphed the sea monster Tiamat into *tehom*, the Hebrew term for "the depths," the primordial sea over which they say that "wind from God" moved "in the beginning." Then, to show that no sea monsters lurked in those primordial waters, the Genesis account says that Israel's God actually "created the great sea monsters"—and did so only *after* he created all the other sea creatures, on the *fifth* day of creation.[65] While the Babylonian story pictures the great sea monster as a *female*, the "mother of all monsters" and of all gods, Hebrew storytellers often speak of Leviathan as male. Others suggest that when God created these sea monsters on the fifth day of creation, he made them, like all the other animals, in pairs: Leviathan, a female monster from the sea, and Behemoth, a male monster from the land—apparently a version of the story that John of Patmos adapted to tell, in his Revelation, how the dragon's two allies emerged, first the "beast from the sea" and then the "beast from the land."

While we think of dragons as creatures of folktales and children's stories, Israel's writers conjured them as images of the forces of disintegration and death that lurk in the background of our world and threaten its stability.[66] Poets and prophets took these images seriously—although not literally—to characterize Israel's enemies in war. When, for example, Psalm 74 praises God for having "crushed the heads of Leviathan" and calls on him to "rise up" again and deliver his people from evil, the anonymous psalmist has in mind the Babylonian soldiers who smashed God's temple and burned it to the ground in the year 586:

> The enemy has destroyed everything in the sanctuary. Your enemies have roared within your holy place. . . . At the upper entrance, they hacked the wooden trellises with axes, and smashed all the carvings with hatchets and hammers; they set Your sanctuary on fire, and desecrated the dwelling of Your holy name.[67]

The prophet Jeremiah, too, grieved and angered by the same war, speaks for Israel as he pictures the king of Babylon as a beast who devours God's people:

> King Nebuchadnezzar of Babylon has devoured me; he has crushed me . . . he has swallowed me like a monster . . . he has spit me out. May my torn flesh be avenged on Babylon![68]

The prophet Ezekiel, a refugee from that same war, mocks Israel's ancient enemy, the king of Egypt—here a stand-in for the Babylonian king who was the prophet's contemporary—as if he were only a sea monster whom Israel's God will haul up and kill like a fish:

> The word of the Lord came to me, saying, Mortal, [say to the] . . . king of Egypt . . . You consider yourself a lion among the nations, but *you are like a dragon in the seas; you thrash about . . . and foul your clear streams.*

Thus says the Lord God . . . I will throw my net over
you . . . haul you up in my dragnet. I will throw you on the
ground, fling you on the open field, and cause . . . the wild
animals of the whole earth to gorge themselves on you.[69]

Exiled in Babylon as a result of the war, Ezekiel pictures God
scattering the dragon's carcass in order to prophesy that God "will
scatter the Egyptians"—that is, the Babylonians—"among the
nations," making them suffer as thousands of Israelites, himself
included, suffered at their hands:

Thus says the Lord God: I am against you, Pharaoh, king
of Egypt, the great dragon . . .
   I will put hooks in your jaws, and make the fish of your
channels stick to your scales, I will fling you into the wilderness. . . . I have given you as food to the animals of the
earth and the birds of the air . . . and I will scatter the
Egyptians among the nations.[70]

The prophet whom scholars call Second Isaiah[71] ironically says
that the Lord must have fallen asleep while the Babylonians were
destroying Israel. Now the prophet calls on the Lord to wake up
and fight, just as ancient stories say he fought the dragon at the
beginning of time:

Awake, awake, put on strength, O arm of the Lord! Awake,
as in days of old, the generations of long ago! Was it not you
who cut Rahab in pieces, who pierced the dragon? Was it
not you who dried up the sea, the waters of the great deep;

who made the depths of the sea a way for the redeemed to cross over?[72]

Yet calling on God to "wake up" and fight the forces of evil acknowledges that destruction and death still wield enormous power. So Isaiah revises the ancient story to suggest that "in the beginning," when God fought the primordial dragon, he failed to actually kill it. Thus Israel's prophets began to project God's battle with Leviathan from the beginning of time to its end, anticipating that, as Isaiah says, "on that day"—the great day at the end of time—finally God will "kill the dragon that is in the sea":

> On that day the Lord with his cruel and great and strong sword will punish Leviathan, the fleeing serpent, Leviathan the twisting serpent, and he will kill the dragon that is in the sea.[73]

How shall this victory be won? Since Isaiah, like other prophets, sees the forces of evil embodied in foreign oppressors, he clings to the hope that God will send a messiah—a king divinely chosen to lead his people to victory. But in his own time, the prophet envisions God's beloved, Israel, as a pregnant woman, crying out in anguish before she gives birth to the promised messiah: "O Lord, we sought you in distress, like a woman who writhes and cries out in labor pains when she is near her time."[74]

John of Patmos was immersed in the prophetic writings, and here he draws upon their images of Israel as a woman and "the nations" as monsters who threaten her, picturing Rome as Isaiah and Ezekiel had envisioned Israel's enemies six hundred years earlier. John reshapes Isaiah's vision of Israel as a woman laboring in childbirth to make it the central drama of his prophecy[75] as he seeks to interpret the struggle that he and other followers of Jesus now face. Convinced that what he believes Isaiah foresaw has now happened—that is, Israel *has* given birth to the messiah, Jesus of Nazareth!—John envisions her as the "woman clothed with the sun," being menaced by a "great red dragon with seven heads and ten horns"[76] that furiously stalks her in order to devour her child the moment he is born. Thus John characterizes the Roman forces that killed Jesus. But John wants to show that despite Rome's apparent success in killing Israel's messiah, Jesus actually escaped, "caught up into heaven," while his mother, Israel, has fled into the wilderness. Now John pictures the dragon, the savage forces embodied in Rome, unleashing its fury on God's people. Raging with frustration at the messiah's escape and sensing his own impending doom, the dragon turns to "make war on . . . her children."[77] Although John apparently envisioned Israel as, in effect, Jesus' "mother," many Christians in later generations have taken the woman "clothed with the sun" as an image of Mary. Such variant interpretations show how John's graphic and evocative images, read in later generations, took on wider resonances.

John probably used such cryptic images because open hostility to Rome could be dangerous; he may have feared reprisal. Other prophets, too, had written in coded language to hold out visions of hope. Nearly two hundred years earlier, for example, the prophet Daniel had challenged his fellow Jews to resist the tyranny of another "evil empire"—or die trying. In 167 b.c.e., the foreign king Antiochus IV, a successor of Alexander the Great, called Epiphanes (literally, "god manifest"), had determined to force Jews under his rule to give up their identity and assimilate into his empire. Living under the pressure of those times, Daniel declared that visions seen in his dreams had shown "four great beasts that came out of the sea," often interpreted as the empires of Babylon, Persia, Greece, and Rome, each more terrifying than the last, the fourth one

> terrifying and dreadful and exceedingly strong. It had great iron teeth . . . and claws of bronze, and was devouring, and breaking in pieces, and stamping what was left with its feet . . . [and had] ten horns on its head.[78]

Daniel says that after receiving this vision, "my spirit was troubled within me, and the visions in my head terrified me. . . . I, Daniel, was overcome and lay sick for some days. . . . I was dismayed by the vision, and did not understand it."[79]

Daniel then says that he was allowed a glimpse into heaven that reassured him that God was about to intervene: "As I watched visions in the night, I saw one who looked like a human being [in Aramaic, 'son of man'] coming with the clouds of heaven." As this man approached God's throne to be presented to the Ancient of Days, he

> was given dominion and glory and kingship, so that all peoples, nations, and languages should serve him: his rule is everlasting, and shall not pass away; his kingdom is one that shall never be destroyed.[80]

When John of Patmos read these words, he, like other followers of Jesus, apparently felt that he *did* understand what Daniel's mysterious vision meant: this shows God investing *Jesus* with power—and shows that Rome, though seemingly invincible, is only a monster bound for destruction. When John says that "the beast that I saw was like a leopard, its feet were like a bear's, and its mouth was like a lion's mouth," he revises Daniel's vision to picture Rome as the worst empire of all, combining the bestial qualities of its predecessors.[81] When he says that the beast's seven heads "are seven kings," John probably means the Roman emperors who ruled from the time of Augustus until his own time.[82] While scholars disagree about precisely *which* emperors John has in mind, John gives an obvious hint: "One of [the beast's] heads seemed to have received a death blow," having been "wounded by the sword, and yet lived."[83]

John's contemporaries would have known that here he refers to an emperor, and some probably would have guessed the emperor Nero, who reigned from 54 to 68 c.e. and was rumored to have been killed by his own sword, although many believed that he had survived. Nero had at first been popular among the Roman people, but stories of his arrogance and cruelty earned him the hatred of many other Romans, especially many senators. After enduring fourteen years of his rule, the senators, on June 8 of the year 68 c.e., declared the emperor a public enemy and sentenced him to be stripped naked, hung up with his head thrust into a huge wooden fork, and publicly beaten to death. The later court historian Suetonius says that the terrified Nero fled Rome on horseback in an undershirt and slippers, his face covered, and hid in a deserted country villa overgrown with weeds and brambles. Hearing that horsemen were approaching to bring him back to Rome, Nero resolved to kill himself. After pleading with his slaves to burn his body so that his enemies could not cut off his head, Nero, his hands shaking, took his dagger and, with the help of his secretary, drove it into his own throat.[84] But since few people could testify that he actually had died, rumors grew that he had escaped to the eastern provinces and someday would return to reclaim his throne.

Although John held all emperors in contempt, he apparently chose Nero—who was said to have burned Jewish followers of Jesus alive to illuminate his garden—to epitomize "the beast" that was Roman rule. To make sure that no one missed his meaning, he offered this telling clue: "This calls for wisdom: let anyone with understanding calculate the number of the beast, for it is the number of a person. Its number is six hundred sixty-six."[85] Historians familiar with the numerological system Jews called gematria, which assigns a numerical value to each letter and calculates the relationship between the numbers, have offered various suggestions to interpret this mysterious number. Some still debate its meaning, but many now agree that the most obvious calculations suggest that the "number of the beast" spells out Nero's imperial name.

John's Book of Revelation, then, vividly evokes the horror of the Jewish war against Rome. Just as the poet Marianne Moore says that poems are "imaginary gardens with real toads in them," John's visions and monsters are meant to embody actual beings and events. John gives plenty of clues to identify the "real toads." As we noted, his vision of a great mountain exploding[86] reflects the eruption of Vesuvius in 79 c.e. The dragon's seven heads suggest the emperors of the Julio-Claudian dynasty, as "the number of the beast" may allude to the hidden name of Nero.

But, one might ask, if that's what he means, why doesn't he just say it? Why does he cloak the actual situations and persons in such elaborate and elusive images? As we noted, this may have to do with the danger of speaking openly against Rome.[87] But John also wants to do more than tell *what happens*; he wants to show *what such events mean*. He wants to speak to the urgent question that people have asked throughout human history, wherever they first imagined divine justice: how long will evil prevail, and when will justice be done? To speak to this question, he invokes the language of the classical prophets, who also sought to assure their people that what happens on earth is neither random nor meaningless, and that the moral complexity of the present world will be sorted out when divine justice sets everything straight and punishes evil. By shifting scenes from earth to heaven and back, John intends to show how events on earth look from God's perspective, until the angel announces that "there shall be no more time"[88] and time is drawn into eternity.

Because John offers his Revelation in the language of dreams and nightmares, language that is "multivalent,"[89] countless people for thousands of years have been able to see their own conflicts, fears, and hopes reflected in his prophecies. And because he speaks from his convictions about divine justice, many readers have found reassurance in his conviction that there *is* meaning in history—even when he does not say exactly what that meaning is—and that there is hope.

John was not the only prophet at the time offering "revelations" warning of divine judgment and announcing the coming end of time. But to John's dismay, the majority of Jews, and later Jesus' Gentile followers as well, would continue to "follow the beast" and to flirt with "the whore" called Babylon, that is, with Rome and its culture. Instead of sharing John's vision of the imminent destruction of the world and preparing for its end, many other followers of Jesus sought ways to live in that world, negotiating compromises with Rome's absolutist government as they sought to sort out, in Jesus' words, what "belongs to Caesar" and what "to God." Realizing this, John decided that he had to fight on two fronts at once: not only against the Romans but also against members of God's people who accommodated them and who, John suggests, became accomplices in evil.[90]

CHAPTER TWO

Visions of Heaven and Hell:
From Ezekiel and John of Patmos to Paul

*A*lthough most people despise you as powerless and insignificant, you are God's beloved, the most important people on earth. As John tells it, when Jesus first appeared he told John to deliver this message to struggling groups of his followers. For John—or, he says, Jesus—is concerned not only about future events but also about what is happening in the present. So even before telling his visions of the end, when the most powerful rulers on earth shall fall from the heights and those now oppressed shall reign victorious with Christ, he opens his Revelation with seven letters meant to transform the way Jesus' followers see themselves right now.

Those who read John's graphic visions into their own lives often hear Jesus addressing them directly in these warnings that John says Jesus dictated to seven "churches." When the Black Death swept over Europe in the fourteenth century, many saw the plague as the arrival of the first horseman of the Apocalypse and prayed to be counted among God's elect.[1] Hundreds of years later, both Catholics and Protestants battling one another in Europe saw themselves as God's saints contending against satanic forces, as did American Christians caught up in the nightmare of the Civil War, those on both sides—the Confederacy and the Union—seeing themselves living in the final days of wrath, fighting for God's truth against evil.[2] Each of those turbulent events drove many people who lived through them to see themselves living in the end-time, and to strive to live as "holy ones," as God's few saints remaining on earth, hoping to enter God's kingdom. Thus in the late nineteenth century, Christians in America calling themselves by such names as Jehovah's Witnesses, Seventh-day Adventists, and members of the Church of Jesus Christ of Latter-day Saints (whom outsiders call Mormons) began to proclaim Christ's imminent return, as many of them still do, offering salvation to those who heed the message and prepare for the coming kingdom. In the twentieth century, even Adolf Hitler, encouraged by his minister of propaganda, Joseph Goebbels, apparently read himself into John's visions, as one divinely chosen to initiate what he proudly called the Third Reich, which suggested not only Germany's third kingdom but also Christ's thousand-year kingdom on earth,[3] while countless others pictured Hitler instead as the furious and diabolical "beast" who makes war on God's people.

The great English poet William Blake wrote that he and his assumed audience "both read the Bible day and night; but you read black where I read white."[4] Conflicting interpretations are not new; even Jesus' earliest known followers—Peter, James, and Paul—apparently read Jesus' *own* message in ways that diverged and sometimes might have clashed. Scholars now realize that only sixty years after Jesus' death, John of Patmos challenged the way others—including many of Paul's followers—were preaching his message. Later generations toned down such disputes and placed both Paul's teaching and John's within what they would come to call the New Testament, which they saw as representing a single and harmonious tradition.

To whom, then, did John write, and what immediate concerns

impelled him to do so? While attacking the Roman enemies, John also challenged enemies within—certain followers of Jesus whom he accused of collaborating with Satan. As Revelation opens, John tells how each of seven small groups living in a cluster of cities on the coast of Asia Minor (again in present-day Turkey)— fruit merchants, weavers, tent makers, cooks, cobblers, slaves, and free persons—suddenly receives a summons from the "King of kings, and Lord of lords." The divine king whose eyes burn like fire dictates letters to John, warning members of these groups that "I know your works"—and how well, or how badly, each one is prepared for the coming cosmic war. Announcing that they have no choice but to take sides before divine wrath destroys the world, John says that the "son of man" has told him to warn each group how they look to God—and what they must do to survive the coming judgment. For instead of writing down his dreams to explore his psyche, John claims that the spirit sent visions to show "what must soon take place." But John wants to do more than *deliver* divine revelation: he wants to persuade his hearers that his visions are genuine—that they show how the world actually looks not to him but to *God*.

John writes as if his visions were unique, sent direct from heaven; and for two thousand years, many Christians have assumed that they were, since his is the only "book of revelation" in the New Testament. But John knew that he was competing with *other* prophets, and was angry that some of his hearers were also listening to them and heeding their messages. John says that "the son of man" ordered him to denounce these lying prophets and warn their followers that he is coming soon to punish—even kill—those who listen to "that woman Jezebel, who calls herself a prophet"[5] and to the man he calls Balaam—John's contemptuous names for the two competitors whose messages clash with his own.

We now know that John was one of many—Jews, Christians, and pagans—speaking in prophecy and writing books of revelation during the early centuries of the Common Era. The 1945 discoveries at Nag Hammadi, in Upper Egypt, where the so-called Gnostic gospels were found, also unearthed dozens of books of revelation,[6] many previously unknown. Before we turn to the questions of who suppressed such revelations and why only *one* such book—that of John of Patmos—came to be included in the New Testament, let's consider what "revelation" meant to John.

John calls the two prophets he denounces *liars*, but his fellow believers probably would have seen him, like them, as traveling prophets who came to speak during worship. How could those listening to such prophets know whom to believe—which visions are genuine and which are false? When Israel's prophets had faced such questions hundreds of years earlier, they often lent credence to their prophecies by telling exactly *where* and *when* a vision had come to them. The prophet Isaiah, for example, wrote that a vision came to him "in the year that King Uzziah died"—742 B.C.E. While he was standing before the altar in the Great Temple in Jerusalem,

> I saw the Lord sitting on a throne, high and lofty; and the hem of his robe filled the temple. Seraphs were attending above him; each had six wings: with two they covered their faces, and with two they covered their feet, and with two they flew. And one called to another and said, "Holy, holy,

holy is the Lord of hosts; the whole earth is full of his glory."[7]

Ezekiel, too, opens his prophecies telling exactly where he was, and when, on the day "the heavens were opened, and I saw visions of God": he was in Babylon (now Iraq) next to the river Chebar, "in the thirtieth year, in the fourth month, on the fifth day of the month,"[8] that is, in 593 B.C.E. Although by that time Babylonian soldiers had demolished the Jerusalem Temple, where, 150 years earlier, Isaiah said he had "seen the Lord," Ezekiel said that *his* vision reassured him that the Lord was still reigning in heaven, since he needed no earthly throne, not even the temple itself. Instead, Ezekiel said, he had seen the Lord enthroned upon a moving chariot of fire, borne on wheels throughout the universe by four winged creatures, with eyes all over their bodies:

> As I looked on the living creatures, I saw a wheel on the earth beside the living creatures, one for each of the four of them. . . .
>
> When they moved, they moved in any one of the four directions. . . . Wherever the spirit would go, they went, and the wheels rose along with them; for the spirit of the living creatures was in the wheels. . . .
>
> When they moved, I heard the sound of their wings like the sound of mighty waters . . . [and] when they stopped, they let down their wings.[9]

Cautioning that words can only approximate what he has seen, and aware that Moses had warned that no one could see God and live,[10] the prophet carefully qualifies what he says he saw ("*something like* a throne, in *appearance like* sapphire; and seated above *the likeness of* a throne was *something that seemed like* a human form"). Hesitating to describe the Divine One, he offers only images of brilliant light.[11]

Fire, sapphire, rainbows, lightning—Ezekiel invokes all of these to suggest "the Lord's *glory*"—in visions have inspired many others to imagine ascending toward the divine throne and wonder what they might see, were they able to approach the "palaces" that housed that throne and enter into God's presence.[12]

When John of Patmos said that he, too, saw "the heavens opened" and was "in the spirit," he wrote visions infused with images drawn from his prophetic predecessors. Like Isaiah and Ezekiel before him, John tells where he was, and on what day, when he first received a vision: "I was on the island called Patmos . . . in the spirit, on the Lord's day."[13] John says that shortly after he was invited to ascend into the heavens, he saw flashes of lightning, dazzling jewels and crystal, rainbows and fire, and heard terrifying bursts of thunder:

> At once I was in the spirit, and there in heaven stood a throne, with one seated on the throne. And the one seated there looks like jasper and carnelian, and around the throne is a rainbow that looks like an emerald. . . .
>
> Coming from the throne are flashes of lightning and rumblings and peals of thunder, and in front of the throne burn seven flaming torches, which are the seven spirits of God; and in front of the throne there is something like a sea of glass, like crystal.

Like Ezekiel, John says he saw four winged beings around the throne, which Isaiah, too, said he had seen there, singing God's praise in words like those Isaiah had heard: "Holy, holy, holy, Lord God almighty, who was, and is, and is to come!"[14]

John of Patmos would have agreed that Jesus of Nazareth, too, received visions, like the stunning vision that Mark's gospel says Jesus saw as he emerged from the Jordan River, dripping with water, after John baptized him. As Mark tells it, at that moment Jesus "saw the heavens torn apart, and the spirit of God descending" upon him and heard a divine voice speaking from heaven, saying, "You are my son, the beloved."[15] No doubt John accepted, too, the widespread reports that many who had known Jesus had "seen the Lord" alive again, just as John said that on that Sunday morning in Patmos, some sixty years after Jesus was crucified, he, too, had seen the one who died and is "alive forever and ever."[16]

John's predecessor, Paul of Tarsus, writing thirty to forty years before John, also claimed that he had "seen the Lord"—an event that left him shocked, stunned, and temporarily blind. As Luke later told it, Paul was traveling to Damascus, the capital city of Syria, to arrest Jesus' followers as traitors to Jewish tradition when suddenly he was struck by a vision that turned his life around. Luke says that Paul saw a blazing light and heard a divine voice as Jesus—who had died decades earlier—challenged him from heaven, demanding, "Why are you persecuting me?"[17] Paul himself said simply that "God revealed his son in me"[18] and sent him as his apostle to the Gentiles, that is, to the non-Jewish population of the Roman Empire. Paul insisted that the risen Jesus had personally revealed to him the distinctive message that he was to preach to these outsiders. As he later wrote to believers in the city of Galatia, in Asia Minor, "I want you to know, brothers, that the gospel I have preached is not of human origin, for I did not receive it from a human source, nor was I taught it, *but I received it through a revelation of Jesus Christ.*"[19]

Paul's impassioned preaching soon attracted a considerable following of Gentiles in the Syrian city of Antioch, but it also embroiled him in bitter disputes with other followers of Jesus. People who belonged to the Jerusalem group led by Jesus' brother James apparently charged that Paul's "gospel" was so radical that it contradicted what they had heard from the most respected leaders, including James himself and the disciples Peter and John. Although what Luke later wrote in the Book of Acts glossed over these disputes, Paul's own words suggest that initially he was concerned that Peter and James—or, at any rate, their followers—might oppose him for preaching to Gentiles a "gospel" that had dropped all Torah requirements,[20] although he says that finally they agreed to let him teach it.

So when other leaders in the movement accused Paul of having no credentials to speak for Jesus, whom he had never met, Paul burst out in anger. He sarcastically called his accusers "super apostles"[21] who were forcing him to talk about matters that made him feel foolish and uncomfortable, since what he had to say would sound like boasting. Paul insisted that he taught only what came to him directly "through revelation"—not from Peter, James, or anyone else on earth. Paul insisted that his authority came straight from God—from "visions and revelations of the Lord."[22]

To validate his claim, Paul, like Isaiah and Ezekiel, mentions a specific time—"fourteen years ago"—when, speaking obliquely, he says that "someone he knew" was "caught up to the third heaven;

whether in the body or out of the body, I do not know; God knows."[23] Repeating these words for emphasis, Paul strongly hints that he himself was "caught up into Paradise."[24] Yet unlike Ezekiel or John of Patmos, who both say that God told them to reveal what they had seen, Paul says that in Paradise he had "heard things that are *not to be told, that no mortal is permitted to repeat.*"[25] While claiming that he has to keep them secret, Paul insists that these "visions and revelations" prove that his message is true, sent from God.

John of Patmos never mentions Paul's name—perhaps, as we shall see, because he remained skeptical of Paul's teaching and kept his distance from those who accepted it.[26] John says that Jesus told him to warn "the saints" in Ephesus that although God has called them to be a holy nation, a "kingdom of priests" like Israel,[27] Satan is actively working through some of them. John says that although gullible people have been taken in by "evildoers" whom they revere as prophets and apostles, Jesus praises those who realize that certain would-be leaders are actually Satan's agents: "I know your works. . . . I know that you cannot tolerate evildoers; *you have tested those who claim to be apostles but are not, and have found them false.*"[28]

For nearly two thousand years, many readers have assumed that John was addressing groups of *Christians undergoing persecution,* and that Jews, as well as Romans, were persecuting them. Since he speaks with distress about those imprisoned and killed "because of the witness to Jesus," many readers assume that John himself experienced persecution. About a hundred years after John wrote, the African convert Tertullian, who actually had seen Christians tortured and killed in a public stadium in his home city of Carthage, speculated that John had been sentenced to death because of his testimony to Jesus, and barely escaped by having been banished instead to the remote island of Patmos, as sometimes happened in the case of condemned prisoners who could claim some social standing.[29]

Many historians today believe that John was not living in a time of active—or, at least, systematic—persecution.[30] Yet John mentions one of Jesus' followers, Antipas, who he says "was killed among you" as a martyr, and expresses concern that others may be arrested, even killed.[31] By the time he was writing, John probably knew, too, that Jesus' own brother James had been killed by a mob in Jerusalem, and that the Roman authorities had killed Peter and Paul. Knowing how such leaders had died, even when such killings didn't happen often, any member of the movement might well fear further reprisals, as John does when he encourages others to "be faithful unto death"[32] should they face mob violence or arrest and execution.

Although John's prophecies are in the New Testament, we do not actually know whether he saw himself as a *Christian*. There is no doubt that John was a devoted follower of Jesus Christ, but he never actually uses the term "Christian"—probably because what we call Christianity had not yet become entirely separate from Judaism. Instead, like Peter, Paul, and other early followers of Jesus, John clearly saw himself *as a Jew who had found the messiah*. Because this placed him among a minority, he also saw himself as part of Israel's "holy remnant," through whom he envisioned that all nations would finally come to share in Israel's blessings.[33] The New Testament Book of Acts says that certain believers did come to be called Christians for the first time just around the time John was writing—but, as we'll see, unlike John, many of them probably were not born Jews.[34]

Writing around 90 c.e., John expresses alarm at seeing God's "holy people" increasingly infiltrated by outsiders who had no regard for Israel's priority. In retrospect, we can see that John stood on the cusp of an enormous change—one that eventually would transform the entire movement from a Jewish messianic sect into "Christianity," a new religion flooded with Gentiles, including Greeks, Asians, Africans, Gauls, Germans, Spaniards, and Egyptians. But since this had not yet happened—not, at least, among the groups John addressed in Asia Minor—he took his stand as a Jewish prophet charged to keep God's people holy, unpolluted by Roman culture. So, John says, Jesus twice warns his followers in Asia Minor to beware of "blasphemers" among them, who "say they are Jews, and are not,"[35] and so have not traditionally belonged among God's people: "I know the slander on the part of those who say they are Jews and are not, but are a synagogue of Satan."[36] Turning to those living in Pergamum, the third-largest city of Asia, crowned by the great temple of Zeus that he calls "Satan's throne," John repeats that Jesus knows that they live in territory dominated by the power of evil: "I know where you are living: where Satan's throne is."[37] Six of the seven cities to which John wrote, in fact, were dominated by imperial temples.[38]

John opposed not only Rome's political and military power but also her cultural influence. Like all people living within a culture they regard as alien and evil, John knew that some contact with outsiders was inevitable. But how much contact is too much? Although John was probably a native of Judea whose first language was Aramaic or Hebrew, he wrote in Greek as a keen observer of the "pagan" behavior he saw all around him.[39] John was worried about contamination, especially since he knew that many Jews tolerated much more compromise than he did. Some, like the wealthy and politically influential Egyptian Jew named Alexander, a contemporary of Jesus, gave up Jewish customs altogether while rising to the highest level of Roman administration; others, like Alexander's nephew Philo, sought to practice Jewish purity laws and religious observance while harmonizing them with Greek philosophic perspectives.[40] Had John met Jews as sophisticated as Philo, he probably would have been repelled by their easy command of Greek and the fine weave of their clothes. Unlike Philo, who praised the magnificent statues and temple to "the god Augustus" that presided over the harbor at Alexandria, his Egyptian home city, John loathed the imperial temple in Pergamum, gleaming with marble and gold, where, he said, "Satan lives."[41]

John may have startled believers who lived in sight of that temple when he implied that some of their most dangerous enemies were not Romans but respected members of their own group. John says that Jesus warns that two prophets among them are actually working for Satan:

> I have a few things against you: you have some there who hold to the teaching of Balaam, who taught Balaak to put a stumbling block before the people of Israel, *so that they would eat food sacrificed to idols, and practice fornication.*[42]

We do not know the real name of the prophet whom John derisively calls Balaam, the biblical name of an evil prophet who sought to deceive Israel; but John accuses this prophet of encouraging idolatry by allowing Jews to eat meat that had been offered in sacrifice to pagan gods and to "practice *porneia*"—sexual impurity.

John says that Jesus also told him to rebuke his followers in the nearby city of Thyatira who listened to another false prophet—and, worse, a woman:

> I have this against you: you tolerate that woman Jezebel, who calls herself a prophet and is teaching and beguiling my servants to practice fornication and to eat food sacrificed to idols. I gave her time to repent, but she refuses to repent of her fornication. Beware, I am throwing her on a bed, and those who commit adultery with her I am throwing into great distress, unless they repent of her doings, and I will strike her children dead.[43]

Since John refuses to speak her real name, much less admit that she is a prophet, he mockingly calls her Jezebel, to associate her with the infamous Canaanite queen who induced her husband, Israel's king, to worship idols and even tried to kill the prophet Elijah.[44]

Are we to take these charges literally—that rival prophets among Jesus' followers actually *were* "seducing [Jesus'] servants to practice fornication" and encouraging them to eat food sacrificed to idols? Here John borrows the sexual metaphor for *idolatry* that prophets like Hosea and Jeremiah used when they scolded their people for "committing adultery" against the Lord, whom they call Israel's "true husband."[45] John clearly understands this language as a prophetic metaphor that warns against consorting with foreign cultures and flirting, so to speak, with foreign gods.

But John also knew that these two issues—eating and sexual activity—aroused conflict whenever Jews discussed whether, or how much, to assimilate. Meat markets in Asia Minor and Greece, as throughout the empire, often sold meat left over from sacrifice in local temples, and government officials distributed such meat to the public to celebrate public holidays and military victories. Families often bought it to serve at dinner parties or to celebrate birthdays, marriages, and funerals.[46] But strictly observant Jews regarded such meat as polluted; the Book of Acts tells how Peter and Jesus' brother James, who shared a concern about purity, mediated arguments among Jesus' followers about whether to eat such "unclean" meat or refuse it.[47]

Arguments about sexual activity could be even more heated. When John accuses "Balaam" and "Jezebel" of inducing people to "eat food sacrificed to idols and practice fornication,"[48] he might have in mind anything from tolerating people who engage in incest to Jews who become sexually involved with Gentiles or, worse, who marry them.[49] Because John wants Jesus' followers to be holy, like the Israel he idealizes, he praises those who scrupulously observe the commandments and reveres those who shun sexual contact altogether, like the 144,000 men who, he says, "have not defiled themselves with women, for they are virgins."[50] The Greek term *parthenos*, here translated as "virgin," does not necessarily mean that these men never had sexual intercourse, but rather that they were practicing sexual abstinence to keep themselves pure, as soldiers in ancient Israel did to prepare for holy war. The number John mentions—twelve thousand from each tribe of his people—suggests that he sees these men as conscripts in God's army, which required each tribe to raise an equal number of soldiers.[51]

John wanted his hearers to keep themselves "holy" like those ancient Israelite soldiers, so that they would be ready to fight on God's side in the coming battle of the end-time. This was not just John's idea. The Dead Sea Scrolls, found in 1947, suggest that some members of the devout sect of Jews often called Essenes (perhaps from the Hebrew *Hasidim*—"holy ones") also practiced celibacy as they waited for the day of judgment. Because of this, Eusebius, the first historian of Christianity, apparently assumed that the Essenes were Christians themselves. Most scholars today think the opposite—that their movement, already established more than fifty years before Jesus' birth, may have influenced how John the Baptist and Jesus of Nazareth preached about the coming end of time.[52] John of Patmos' contemporary Josephus, a Jewish historian, investigated the Essenes when he was sixteen years old and later wrote that some of their most devoted members lived in a communal settlement at Qumran, on the Dead Sea, each having signed over his property to the community and having sworn to live by a common rule, observing strict guidelines to maintain purity while washing, dressing, working, and worshipping in common. The strictest among them, like the "holy ones" John most admired, practiced celibacy.[53]

Besides separating from outsiders socially and sexually, some Essenes sought to separate financially as well, or at least to limit their financial dealings with them. John, too, associates commerce with idolatrous worship and savagely caricatures "the beast from the land" for trying to force everyone to worship its master and to require that everyone who buys or sells bear the mark of the beast—that is, "the name of the beast, or the number of its name."[54] We do not know exactly what John had in mind. This mark may have been an imperial stamp required on official documents, or perhaps a tattoo on the body authorizing people to engage in business or participate in trade guilds that required members to pour libations to the gods or offer grain to their statues. John might also have had in mind the images and names of Roman emperors and gods stamped on coins, which he and other devout Jews bitterly resented. Some refused to handle or touch such coins, insisting that even looking at such demonic images implicated one in idolatry. John apparently wants God's "holy ones" to boycott economic contact with Rome altogether, since he warns that anyone who receives the mark of the beast—whether this means accepting an imperial stamp, joining a trade guild, or even handling Roman money—shall

> drink the wine of God's wrath, poured unmixed into the
> cup of his anger, and they will be tormented with fire and
> sulfur in the presence of the holy angels and of the Lamb . . .
> forever and ever.[55]

Because the Essenes, like John, saw the Romans as God's enemies, the latest incarnation of evil, they saw themselves at war with Rome. Most historians have assumed that, like John, they were speaking of "holy war" only *metaphorically*, since their movement began about a hundred years before the actual outbreak of war in 66 C.E. Recently, however, British scholar Richard Bauckham has suggested that the Essenes may have been preparing for actual war—stockpiling weapons, engaging in military exercises, and training their "holy ones" to fight as soldiers.[56] Bauckham points out that their Scroll of the War of the Sons of Light Against the Sons of Darkness, which pictures the final battle between good and evil, sketches out what may be an actual war plan, specifying how to station soldiers, what to inscribe on their weapons, at what distance from the camp to build latrines, and how to bury the dead. Archaeological remains at their settlement show that when the war reached its climax, after the Romans achieved victory around 70 c.e., they treated the Essenes as enemy combatants, first besieging and capturing their settlement, then slaughtering everyone who lived there.

When John of Patmos speaks of holy war, however, rather than urging God's "holy ones" to prepare for actual combat, he pictures Jesus as a warrior king storming down from heaven, leading armies of angels, thus suggesting that God needs no human army. When John says that Jesus urges his "holy ones" to *conquer*, he apparently expects them to "conquer" as he says Jesus did—by bearing witness to God "unto death." And while they await this final battle, John urges them to remain *holy*—sexually, socially, and religiously.

When John accuses "evildoers" of leading gullible people into sin, what troubles him is what troubled the Essenes: whether—or how much—to accommodate pagan culture. And when we see Jesus' earliest followers, including Peter, James, and Paul, not as we usually see them, as *early Christians*, but as they saw themselves—as *Jews who had found God's messiah*—we can see that they struggled with the same question. For when John charges that certain prophets and teachers are encouraging God's people to eat "unclean" food and engage in "unclean" sex, he is taking up arguments that had broken out between Paul and followers of James and Peter about forty years earlier—an argument that John of Patmos continues with a second generation of Paul's followers.[57] For when we ask, who are the "evildoers" against whom John warns? we may be surprised at the answer. Those whom John says Jesus "hates" look very much like *Gentile followers of Jesus converted through Paul's teaching*. Many commentators have pointed out that when we step back from John's angry rhetoric, we can see that the very practices John denounces are those that Paul had recommended.[58]

Ever since Paul had preached as "apostle to the Gentiles," around 50 to 66 c.e. in towns throughout Asia Minor, Greece, and Syria, he and his followers had advocated practices quite different from John's. When converts in the Greek city of Corinth had asked Paul about meat offered in sacrifice at pagan temples, for example, Paul wrote back that since "we know no idol in the world really exists,"[59] eating sacrificial meat could not do any harm. Perhaps as an afterthought, he added that the only possible harm might be to offend "the weak"—that is, people who don't understand that pagan gods don't exist and so regard such meat as "unclean"—perhaps including rigorous and observant Jews like John.[60]

What about "unclean" sexual relationships, like marriages between believers and outsiders? When Paul's converts had raised this question, he advised them not to seek divorce, since Jesus had forbidden it, adding that such marriages could benefit unbelieving partners, perhaps even recruit pagan husbands.[61] Since the groups Paul addressed consisted primarily of Gentiles, strictly observant Jews like John could have inferred that he sanctioned mixed marriages, which some of them called "uncleanness." The prophets John derisively calls by the biblical names of despised Gentile outsiders—Balaam and Jezebel—are likely to be *Gentile converts to Paul's teaching.* What apparently upset John of Patmos, then, is that forty years after Paul's death, he still heard of those he called "false prophets" giving advice that sounded suspiciously like Paul's— telling Jesus' followers that it didn't matter whether they ate sacrificial meat or engaged in mixed marriages. And although Paul actually directed this relaxed teaching about Torah observance primarily toward *Gentile converts,* his letters show that intense— sometimes bitter—disputes over such matters had divided Jesus' followers from the start.

Since John of Patmos adhered closely to Jewish tradition, and perhaps emigrated from Jerusalem, he may have personally known James, Jesus' brother who had become a leader among Jesus' followers there. In any case, John would have admired James' reputation for being an observant Jew, which had earned him the nickname "James the righteous." But in those early years, as we have seen, trouble broke out when the maverick called Paul of Tarsus came out of nowhere and began to preach a "gospel" quite different from what was taught in James' and Peter's circle.

Some readers may be surprised to hear of disagreement among the apostles, since many have read what Luke later wrote in the Book of Acts to gloss over this embarrassing episode. Luke pictures Peter and James inviting Paul to an "apostolic council" to discuss whether Jesus' Gentile followers should follow some purity observances, and pictures Peter proposing a gentlemanly compromise, then closing the meeting as he and James part from

Paul "in peace."[62] But about thirty years *before* Luke wrote this version, Paul had sent a blunt and angry letter about a dispute with Peter to believers in the city of Galatia, in Asia Minor. As we've seen, while Paul admitted that he'd never met Jesus during his lifetime, nor had he ever been one of his followers—that, on the contrary, as a devout Jew, he had been their enemy—he insisted that Jesus, *after* his death, had appeared to him. As we've noted, Paul says that this revelation, which "the living Jesus" sent to him straight from heaven, completely changed his life. Convinced that God "called me so that I might proclaim [Christ] among the Gentiles,"[63] Paul gave up his earlier scruples against contact with Gentiles and began to live among them and even share their "unclean" food, while preaching "his gospel" as an independent missionary based in the Syrian city of Antioch.

After three difficult years in Asia Minor and Greece, Paul says he went to Jerusalem to visit Peter and stayed for two weeks, during which he met Jesus' brother James. Fourteen years after that, Paul says, he went back to Jerusalem with Barnabas, apparently to get the approval of James, Peter, and John, whom he calls the "recognized leaders," and "privately . . . laid before them the gospel that I preach among the Gentiles, in order to make sure that I was not running, or had not run, in vain."[64] This time Paul brought the Greek convert Titus with him, apparently to help make the case that such Gentiles need not be circumcised to join "God's people." Paul says that James, Peter, and John finally agreed to not require such Gentiles to be circumcised and consented to what he was teaching Gentiles.

Yet apparently they had not reached clear agreement about dietary and sexual practices, for Paul says that "when Peter came to Antioch, I opposed him to his face, because he stood condemned by his own actions."[65] Paul explains that when Peter first arrived in Antioch, he had gone along with Paul's practice of eating with Gentile converts. But after members of James' group arrived from Jerusalem, Peter, either fearing or giving in to their criticism, stopped eating "unclean" food. At that point, Paul wrote, he challenged Peter in public, calling him a hypocrite, and insisted, contrary to what others taught, that "the gospel" does not require Gentiles—and apparently not Jews like Peter, either—to practice what observant Jews regarded as purity in matters of food or sex.[66]

But when Paul heard that James' followers had scolded his converts in Galatia, telling them that their teacher didn't understand—much less teach—the *true* gospel of Jesus, Paul attacked. Furious, he rebuked his former followers for turning on him:

> I am astonished that you are so quickly deserting the one who called you in the grace of Christ, and are turning to a different gospel! Not that there *is* a different gospel, but *there are some who are confusing you, and want to pervert the gospel of Christ.*[67]

When some protested that followers of James, Jesus' own brother, and Peter, his closest disciple, had authorized "the gospel" they now accepted, Paul replied that it made no difference *who* contradicted what he had taught. He cursed whoever it was—even an angel from heaven! Paul twice repeats this solemn curse:

> Even if we—or an angel from heaven—should proclaim a gospel contrary to what we proclaimed to you, let that one

be accursed! As we have said before, so now I repeat, if anyone proclaim to you a gospel contrary to what you received,
let that one be accursed![68]

When forced to defend himself and his message, then, Paul does
what other prophets and visionaries did: appeal to a higher
authority that he said came to him "by revelation"—although not
everyone accepted his claim.

Some forty years after that dispute, when John of Patmos met
with groups of Jesus' followers throughout Asia Minor, he was
dismayed to discover considerable variation among them. John
found some groups, perhaps predominantly Jewish, that adhered
closely to Jewish tradition and welcomed him as a respected
prophet. Having found such a group in the city of Philadelphia,
John wrote that Jesus praised them and promised to "write on you
the name of my God, and the name of . . . the new Jerusalem that
comes down . . . from heaven, and my own new name."[69] But John
also encountered groups of believers, many of them Gentiles, who
apparently had accepted "Paul's gospel"—and clashed with them.
Those John encountered in the decade of the 90s belonged, of
course, to the second generation of Paul's converts, since it was
about thirty years since "the great apostle" had preached there.
Yet ever since Paul had worked in Ephesus and neighboring cities,
groups devoted to his teaching had sprung up throughout the
region, attracting an increasing number of Gentiles from the places
we know today as Syria, Turkey, Africa, and Lebanon.[70]

As John saw it, Paul's converts were not like the Gentiles
whom Jews had called "those who show reverence for God" and
who had long sought to join with them to worship their God.

Those old-fashioned Gentiles had known their place, keeping a respectful distance from those born Jews, since they realized that gaining full access to the Jewish community would require them to change their whole way of life. Men would have had to undergo surgery to become circumcised; both men and women would have had to adopt sexual, social, and dietary practices that would separate them from their former families and friends before they could qualify to join God's holy people.

By contrast, some of Paul's converts were saying that, having been "baptized into Jesus Christ,"[71] they were as good as those born Jews—maybe even better. John, who sees Israel's privilege linked to the obligation to remain "holy," is angry that they claim to belong to Israel while ignoring what the Torah requires. To justify such negligence, these "would-be Jews" invoke the authority of the famous—or, John may have felt, infamous—missionary Paul, self-professed "apostle to the Gentiles."

Even worse, from John's point of view, is that instead of respecting Israel's priority, such newcomers speak of *themselves*—and Gentiles of every kind—*as if they themselves were Jews*, claiming both Israel's name and her prerogatives. John seems to have such people in mind when he says that Jesus told him to tell his people in Philadelphia that "those who say they are Jews, and are not, but are lying," are nothing but a "synagogue of Satan."[72] John adds that Jesus assures his true followers in Smyrna that he knows what slander such people sling at them: "I know the slander on the part of *those who say they are Jews and are not, but are a synagogue of Satan.*"[73]

But, some readers may ask, when John attacks the "synagogue of Satan," isn't he talking about *actual* Jews, that is, members of local synagogues who are hostile to Christians? When he warns *"those who say they are Jews and are not,"* doesn't he mean the *opposite* of what he says—that they actually *are* Jews, but Jews who don't *deserve* to be called by that name? Many—perhaps most— scholars accepted this convoluted interpretation in the past, since only this reading could fit what most of them took for granted— namely, that John, although probably Jewish by birth, had become a *Christian* by the time he wrote this book.[74] Many have also assumed what one well-informed scholar recently repeated: that "Judaism and Christianity would probably have been separated by this time,"[75] that is, around 90 C.E.

Christian scholars have long taken for granted the common- place—most often unspoken—assumption that "Judaism," as a living, ongoing, and powerful tradition, effectively came to an end around 70 C.E., when the Jerusalem Temple was destroyed. Since Christians tend to assume that Judaism was only a preparation for Christianity, many used to date the beginning of what they called "the Christian Era" from the temple's destruction. The influential scholar David Aune, who has written three enor- mously learned volumes of commentary on the Book of Revela- tion, is aware that John's language and themes indicate that he is Jewish, yet he regards him as undeniably Christian. Aune tries to resolve the apparent contradiction by noting that John's lifetime spanned this supposed transition. Thus he suggests that John was "a Jewish-Christian prophet who had moved from Judaism to Christianity at some point in his career."[76]

Today, however, some scholars are questioning assumptions like these, which project onto John's biography what many Chris- tians would later envision as the divinely guided course of history, which they picture "progressing" (as Aune says John himself "progressed") from Judaism to Christianity. But once we step back from this interpretation to reflect that John was writing during the first century—before the invention of "Christianity," so to speak—we can see that what he writes does not support this view. John not only sees himself as a Jew but regards being Jewish as an honor that those who fail to observe God's covenant—especially non-Jews—do not deserve. For *if John knows the term "Christian," he never mentions it, much less applies it to himself.* Instead, as we have seen, John, like Peter, James, and virtually all of Jesus' earliest followers, for that matter, consistently sees himself *as a Jew who acknowledges Jesus as Israel's messiah*—not someone who has converted to a new "religion."

Roman magistrates may have been the first, in fact, to coin the term "Christian," specifically for the purpose of identifying *Gentiles* who aroused suspicion of treason against Rome, as well as atheism, because after receiving baptism they abruptly stopped worshipping the traditional gods.[77] One alert and cautious governor in Asia Minor, named Pliny, investigating charges that certain people in his region had stopped worshipping the gods, discovered something suspicious: these people had done so only *after* they joined the cult devoted to Jesus of Nazareth. Around the year 112, Pliny had ordered the arrest of some people whom he, like other magistrates, called "Christians" and reported to the emperor what he learned from interrogating them and torturing two women slaves. Pliny wrote to the emperor Trajan that the accused often met early in the morning to "pray to Jesus as a god" and that even when facing the death penalty, some had refused to pour a cup of wine to honor the gods or the emperor's statue.

While admitting that "I do not know whether they were guilty of other criminal acts," Pliny explained that he had sent them off to be executed, deciding that "because of their obstinacy alone," they well deserved it—a decision that Trajan quickly approved.[78]

What aroused such magistrates' suspicion, however, were acts that would come to their attention *only* in the case of people who previously *had* worshipped the gods. Since Roman rulers already regarded Jews as "atheists" so far as their gods were concerned, for the most part they followed the policy of treating Jews as legally tolerated "atheists." Since magistrates did not expect them to perform pagan sacrifices, Jews who followed Jesus would have escaped their notice, unless, like Peter, they were known leaders or, like Paul, they proved to be public nuisances. In most cases, then, when Jesus' followers aroused popular hostility and came to the magistrates' attention, they were *Gentile converts*. Luke wrote in his Book of Acts that Jesus' followers "were first called *Christians* at Antioch,"[79] the capital city of Syria, suggesting that these were people who had joined the movement after hearing Paul preach among Gentiles there, probably around 50 to 65 c.e.[80]

But, we might ask, would John have spoken so bitterly—or say that Jesus had—about converts to Paul's "gospel" that he could call some of them a "synagogue of Satan"? Many of John's readers find this hard to imagine. In the first place, many Christians today think of Paul's teaching simply as what Christianity is. Many also assume that because Paul and John are both Jesus' followers, they surely would have agreed with each other. And many have accepted Luke's account, which suggests that even though James and Peter found Paul's message startlingly radical, they had, in effect, agreed to disagree or, at least, to accept his preaching to non-Jews. Yet even when Luke spins the story as he does in the Book of Acts, he says that the apostolic council headed by Peter and James concluded that Gentile converts should observe at least *some* traditional guidelines—for example, they should eat only meat butchered in a traditionally Jewish way and "avoid fornication."[81] Paul himself had set no such conditions, writing instead to his followers in Rome that Gentiles could be "grafted on" to God's people simply by professing faith in Jesus and receiving baptism.[82]

Did Paul, then, actually encourage Gentile converts to think of themselves as Jews, as John suggests, or even *better than* Jews? Almost certainly not. On the contrary, his letters show that he often warned Gentiles not to "boast."[83] But the fact that he had to repeat this warning so often shows that he found many Gentiles who *did* boast that they were superior to Jews. Frustrated as he was with them, Paul may have realized that his own words had encouraged Gentiles to think of themselves as being, spiritually speaking, the *real* Jews. In his widely circulated Letter to the Romans, for example, Paul had written that

> *a person is not a Jew who is one outwardly,* nor is true circumcision something external and physical. Rather, *a person is a Jew who is one inwardly, and real circumcision is a matter of the heart—spiritual, not literal.* Such a person receives praise not from human beings, but from God.[84]

Much of what Paul wrote, in fact, could be read—and *has* been read ever since—to mean that God *disinherited the Jewish people in favor of Gentile believers,* whom Paul calls the "spiritual Israel," by contrast with those whom he calls "my kindred according to the flesh, who are Israelites,"[85] who belong "to Israel according to the flesh." In his Letter to the Romans, Paul writes that "not all who are from Israel *are* Israel; not all who are Abraham's seed are his children," since *"it is not the children of the flesh who are God's children, but the children of the promise."*[86] Writing to Gentile believers in Galatia, Paul assures them that although they were not born Jews, now that "you belong to Christ, *you are Abraham's seed,* heirs according to the promise"—children of Abraham "born according to the spirit . . . like Isaac."[87] Paul concludes this letter by blessing all those who belong to the "spiritual Israel," which he calls "the Israel of God."[88]

By the time John of Patmos traveled to Asia Minor, then, he found many followers of Paul who apparently assumed that even groups consisting largely of Gentile converts had now, in effect, *become* Israel. No wonder, then, that when John heard of such people who "say they are Jews, and are not, but are lying," he found their claims outrageous. Although he does not deny their relationship to Jesus, he derisively suggests that they belong to "Satan's synagogue" and longs for the day when Jesus shall return to set them straight. For John reassures those who really *are* Jews that Jesus has promised that when he comes back,

> I will make those of the synagogue of Satan, who say they are Jews and are not, but are lying—*I will make them come and bow down before your feet, and they will learn that I have loved you!*[89]

Distressed as he was by such people, John could hardly have imagined what he might have seen as the greatest identity theft of all time: that eventually Gentile believers not only would call themselves Israel but would claim to be the *sole rightful heirs* to the legacy of God's chosen people. Nor did John foresee that Paul's "gospel," which adapted Jesus' message for Gentiles, would soon overflow the movement to create, in effect, a *new religion*.

What John of Patmos preached would have looked old-fashioned—and simply wrong—to Paul's converts in such cities as Ephesus and in Syrian Antioch, which eventually became the center of the Pauline circle.[90] The first person we know who aggressively called himself "a Christian" to distinguish himself from Jews was the Syrian convert Ignatius of Antioch. Converted to Paul's message perhaps around 80 or 90 c.e.,[91] twenty to thirty years after "the great apostle" first preached in his home city, Ignatius so zealously took this message to heart that he took Paul as the model for his own life. Calling himself Christophoros, "Christ bearer," this strong-minded believer traveled through Asia Minor about fifteen years after John had been there and, like John, wrote letters to seven churches near the coast, including three to groups of Jesus' followers in Ephesus, Smyrna, and Philadelphia—the same cities that John had addressed.

Like John, Ignatius identified with people who suffered persecution. Claiming the name "Christian," in fact, would cost him his life. For, after declaring himself a Christian before a Roman magistrate, he was sentenced to die horribly, consigned "to the beasts"—to be torn apart by wild animals in a public spectacle. In one of the messages he sent while being transported from Syria to

Rome for execution, he complained that he was "chained to ten leopards," the hostile soldiers who guarded him. When the convoy stopped at night while moving through Asia Minor, other Christians bribed the guards in order to meet with him, bringing food and providing him with the means to send letters. Writing a famous— some say fanatical—letter to Jesus' followers in Rome, where he was to die, Ignatius pleaded with them to not intervene or help him escape, declaring that he passionately hoped to "die for God":

> I am writing to all the churches, and I tell all people this, that I am willing to die for God—if you do not prevent it. I beg you, do not try to be "kind" to me. *Let me be eaten by the beasts, through whom I can reach God. I am God's wheat, and the teeth of wild animals shall grind me, so that I may become God's pure bread.* . . . Plead with Christ for me . . . that I may become a sacrifice.[92]

Apparently Ignatius got his wish and died in a bloody struggle before a shouting crowd in the Roman Colosseum around the year 110.[93]

Because Ignatius and John both saw themselves as leaders among Jesus' followers, commentators often have assumed that they taught and believed the same things. Yet when we look more closely, we can see that each upheld a different vision of who "God's people" are—and who should be their leaders. The differences between John's groups and Ignatius', then, also involved power struggles. Had anyone asked both John and Ignatius who should lead Jesus' followers? Both, no doubt, would have said the same thing: *Jesus Christ himself*. But since both lived two to three generations after Jesus' death, when pressed to say who should succeed Jesus as leader now, each would have answered differently. John, who envisioned Jesus' followers as outposts of Israel, believed that these groups, like Israel, while divinely guided by angels, should *humanly* be led by prophets like himself. Ignatius, on the other hand, adopted what Paul taught: that God had appointed as leaders "apostles first, prophets second."[94] Ignatius believed, too, that the apostles, in turn, had designated "bishops" ("supervisors" in Greek) and "priests" ("elders" in Greek).[95]

Unlike John, who saw himself as a prophet, Ignatius identified himself as a "supervisor," or bishop, nothing less than "the bishop of Syria," as if he were the sole rightful leader of all Christians in Syria. When some people objected and accused him of acting as if he were an apostle, Ignatius replied indignantly that "I am not giving orders like an apostle"; he claimed only to be one of their designated successors. Ignatius was the first, so far as we know, to actively promote—and represent—this new system of leadership. Writing to Jesus' followers in Asia Minor, Ignatius insisted that every real "church" must have a bishop, as well as priests and deacons: "without these, nothing can be called a church!"[96]

Yet these could be fighting words among groups led by prophets like John. John never mentions "bishops" at all. The only "apostles" whom John reveres are Jesus' twelve disciples, "the twelve apostles of the Lamb,"[97] whom he envisions in heaven. When John hears of certain people still alive who are promoting themselves as "apostles" in Ephesus, he responds with alarm. He congratulates Jesus' followers in Ephesus for having met them with suspicion, first testing them, then rejecting them as frauds and "evildoers": "*I know that you cannot tolerate evildoers; you have tested those who say they are apostles and are not, and have found them to be false.*"[98] John may have suspected that such would-be apostles were coming from Pauline circles, where believers called apostles often presided, trying to enter established groups and take them over.

Ignatius, for his part, knew of groups like John's, led by prophets, and fiercely campaigned against them. Whether Ignatius knew of John of Patmos and his prophecies we do not know, since he never mentions him by name.[99] But when he visited Jesus' followers in the city of Philadelphia, in Asia Minor, at first he trod carefully, anticipating opposition. Although he was hoping to establish a new kind of leadership there, Ignatius knew that Philadelphia had been famous for its active prophets from the time when the apostle Philip's four daughters, all prophets, had lived there to the time when John of Patmos had found in Philadelphia a strong following, as had the respected female prophet Ammia.[100]

Instead of challenging prophetic authority when visiting Philadelphia, Ignatius apparently decided to *claim it himself.* He writes that while he was worshipping with Jesus' people there, suddenly the spirit of God came upon him and he shouted out in worship, as inspired prophets did: "I cried out when I was with you; I cried out in a loud voice—God's own voice!" But what Ignatius says God impelled him to shout was not what his hearers expected but what he preached all the time: "*Pay attention to the bishop, the priests, and the deacons!*" Ignatius admits that some people who heard him objected, charging that rather than speaking "in the spirit" Ignatius had faked it, having been told in advance that members of that congregation looked on bishops and priests with suspicion. Ignatius denies that anyone had told him anything and swears by God that

> I did not learn this from any human source. *It was the spirit that kept on speaking in these words.* . . . *Do nothing apart from the bishop* . . . *prize unity; avoid schism; imitate Jesus Christ.*[101]

Despite his claim of speaking in prophecy, and the cautious respect he expresses for ancient prophets, when Ignatius later writes to believers in Philadelphia, he rejects what John and the gospel writers take for granted—that what validates faith in Jesus are "the Scriptures" of the Hebrew Bible, especially its prophecies. Thus the Gospel of Mark opens with Isaiah's oracle of a "voice crying in the wilderness"[102] to suggest that Isaiah prophesied the coming of John the Baptist; and the Gospel of Matthew prefaces every episode, where possible, with passages from the oracles of Isaiah, Jeremiah, and Zechariah, as well as the Psalms of David, to show that these foretold the events that happened through Jesus. As we've seen, John of Patmos, too, saturated what he wrote with allusions to the prophecies of Isaiah, Jeremiah, Ezekiel, and Daniel.[103]

Ignatius, by contrast, hardly ever cites passages from the Hebrew Scriptures and argues with believers who regard them as the primary, or "ancient," sources (in Greek, *ta archaia*): "I have heard some people say, 'If I don't find it in *the primary sources,* I don't believe in what is preached as gospel.'"[104] On the contrary, Ignatius declares, the primary sources are not the Hebrew Scriptures but what he finds in Paul's letters: "for me, the primary sources are [Christ's] cross, his resurrection, and the faith that comes through him."[105]

Against those who insist on going back to what "is written" in the Hebrew Scriptures, Ignatius defends his own teaching by saying, "but it *is* written"—written, that is, in Paul's letters. His opponents could reply that Paul's letters don't count, since they aren't "the Scriptures"—and would not be officially regarded as such, by most Christians, for generations to come.[106] Yet declaring that his own faith is founded upon "[Christ's] cross, his resurrection, and the faith that comes through him," Ignatius demands a radical break with the Jewish past: "If anyone interprets Judaism to you, do not listen to him." What matters now, he declares, is *Christianity*, not Judaism.[107]

Like many converts, then, Ignatius sharply marked off his new life "in Christ" from his pagan past. Besides adopting the term "Christian," he was the first among Jesus' followers, so far as we know, to claim this name for himself and to use the term "Christianity." He may have even coined this word, perhaps to show his family and neighbors that he had not simply joined what he saw as an inferior provincial cult called Judaism. Ignatius apparently regarded people like John, who validated the gospel through the Hebrew Scriptures, as foolishly—and fatally—mistaken, for he goes so far as to say that "whoever is not called by this [new] name [Christian] does not belong to God!"[108]

Although Ignatius claims to belong to the new "Israel," he does not claim to be a Jew. In fact, his writings played a key role in *reversing* how Christians thought about Jewish tradition. Unlike Christians who validated their "gospels" through testimonies from the Hebrew Scriptures, Ignatius accuses those who "introduce

Judaism" of heresy! Yet while repudiating "Judaism," this Syrian convert was so convinced that he and other "Christians" had taken on Israel's identity that he urged his fellow believers to avoid offending "the Gentiles," as if he actually were Jewish himself. Eventually, as we know, John of Patmos would be seen by the majority of his readers as a *Christian*, after members of that movement posthumously adopted him—along with Paul, the disciples, and Jesus himself—into what some would call a "new race," neither Jewish nor Gentile but a "third race" called *Christians*.[109]

Thus, what began among devout Jews—Jesus, Paul, James, Peter, and John of Patmos—within forty to fifty years had ignited a new movement that would claim to supplant Jewish tradition. Paul, who had described himself as "an Israelite, a descendant of Abraham, a member of the tribe of Benjamin"[110]—believing that a revelation from Jesus required him to open the gospel message to "the nations," as Jews called Gentiles—succeeded in translating it into terms they could understand and practice. But during the decades after Paul's death in 65 C.E., as the movement that would become "Christianity" increasingly attracted crowds of newcomers, most of them Gentiles, Paul's version proved powerfully influential. Eventually, it would eclipse or at least modify what his predecessors had taught.

Whose revelations, then, are genuine—Paul's or those of John of Patmos? The future of the movement would turn on this question—or, more accurately, on which would gain acceptance as "canonical." As we shall see, two hundred years later, influential Christian leaders chose *both* and wrestled them into the same New Testament canon. But we now know that during those turbulent years, some leaders suppressed an astonishing range of *other* "revelations" that Christians throughout the empire read and treasured. Who made those decisions, and why? How did John of Patmos' "revelation" come to trump so many others and become the only one included in the New Testament? To these questions we now turn.

CHAPTER THREE

Other Revelations: Heresy or Illumination?

In times of distress, driven beyond ordinary endurance, we may find ourselves asking how—or whether—we can survive. The historian Norman Cohn suggests that people living in social or political crisis often become increasingly preoccupied with the "end-times," just as John of Patmos began to write in the aftermath of the Jewish war.[1] As war, uprisings, and economic turmoil threatened the stability of the Roman Empire, countless other people—Jews, pagans, and Christians—produced a flood of "revelations," many only recently discovered.

Yet crises occur in every generation and, for that matter, in every lifetime; and those who survive them often speak of insights that have nothing to do with the "end-times." From the first century to the present, certain people have told how, in crisis, they suddenly, unexpectedly, experience God's presence—or some presence—offering hope. The psychiatrist Viktor Frankl, writing of his time spent in a Nazi death camp, tells how, for a moment, he vividly experienced his wife's presence, although he didn't know whether she was alive or dead. He relates, too, a conversation with a dying young woman whose sanity at first he questioned when she told him that the tree outside was speaking to her, saying, "I am life—eternal life."[2]

At the beginning of the twentieth century, the psychologist William James recounted many accounts of spiritual breakthrough, including his own recovery from depression, in his book *The Varieties of Religious Experience*. James relates some experiences that are strikingly similar to those found in *other* ancient "books of revelation" not included in the New Testament. Some, like the Revelation of Peter and the Revelation of Paul, have been known for centuries; but the find at Nag Hammadi, which included the Gospel of Thomas, contains about twenty writings that offer "revelations," many of them very different from John's Revelation—even one that claims to be John's *secret* book of revelation. Although these other books sometimes are titled "Apocryphon" ("something secret") rather than "Apocalypsis," the titles often were added later. The title of John's book can be called "apocalypse" or "revelation," depending on whether one translates from Greek or Latin. Such books claim to reveal divine secrets, although not necessarily about the end of the world. Historian Elliot Wolfson defines "apocalyptic" as "the revelation of divine mysteries through . . . visions, dreams, and other paranormal states of consciousness."[3]

The Revelation of Zostrianos, written about fifty years after John of Patmos wrote, and found at Nag Hammadi in 1945, tells how the young Zostrianos, tormented by questions and overwhelmed by suicidal depression, walked alone into the desert. Finding no place "to rest my spirit . . . since I was deeply troubled and despairing," Zostrianos says he had resolved to kill himself. But as he stood alone, steeling himself to do so, he says that suddenly he became aware of a being radiating light, who "said to me, 'Zostrianos . . . have you gone mad?'"[4] This divine presence, Zostrianos said, "rescued [me] from the whole world," released him from despair, and offered illumination. Then, Zostrianos says, "*I realized that the power in me was greater than the darkness, because it contained the whole light.*"[5]

The Revelation of Peter, found with the others in 1945, also opens in a desperate moment. Peter says that he was standing in the temple with other disciples when "I saw the priests and the people running up to us with stones, as if they would kill us. And I was afraid that we were going to die." Terrified, he says, he heard Jesus tell him to "put your hands . . . over your eyes, and say what you see." Peter says:

> but when I had done it, I did not see anything. I said, "There is nothing to see." Again he told me, "Do it again." And fear came over me, [and] joy, for I saw a new light greater than the light of day. Then it came down upon the Savior, and I told him what I saw. [6]

Startled by visions that others reported after Jesus' death, some Christians found that they, too, could communicate with him, as John of Patmos had—so these "books of revelation" claim. Although such revelations might not change outward circumstances—Peter's life actually *was* in danger, and tradition tells us that, just as he feared, he was caught and crucified—the Revelation of Peter suggests that what Jesus revealed enabled him to face his death with courage and hope.

Like John of Patmos' Revelation, these other "revelations," written several generations after Jesus' death, were not the work of the original disciples. Instead, followers of Jesus who chose to remain anonymous wrote many of them under the names of disciples—not to deceive their readers but to show that they were writing "in the spirit" of those whose names they borrowed. Furthermore, many of these sources are probably not written by

Christians at all. Writings like Thunder, Perfect Mind and the Discourse on the Eighth and Ninth draw upon sacred traditions of Egypt and Greece and, in some cases, on the Hebrew Bible as well.[7] Some, like Allogenes, might combine Jewish esoteric teaching and Greek philosophic concepts with practices similar to Buddhist meditation techniques. These diverse sources offer various ways to engage in spiritual practice—some of which go far beyond what we find in familiar Jewish and Christian scriptures. Those who wrote and loved such "revelations" acknowledged that, besides the canonical Scriptures, available to everyone, there were also *secret* writings containing advanced teaching to be shared only with "the wise."

One such writer is the Jewish prophet Salathiel, a contemporary of John of Patmos, who would have recognized him as a kindred spirit, even though Salathiel was not a follower of Jesus. Like other prophets, Salathiel opens his revelation telling *when* and *where* he first received revelations:

> In the thirtieth year after the destruction of our city, I, Salathiel, who am also called Ezra, was in Babylon. I was troubled as I lay on my bed, and my thoughts welled up in my heart, because I saw the desolation of Zion. . . . My spirit was greatly agitated, and I began to speak anxious words to the Most High.[8]

Salathiel explains that he, like John, was devastated by the war that had destroyed Jerusalem and was writing around the same time, during the decade of the 90s c.e. The author, who calls himself Salathiel ("I asked God"),[9] adopted the pen name Ezra to show that he was writing what he called the Revelation of Ezra (often called the Fourth Book of Ezra) in the spirit of the great Jewish leader who, 550 years earlier, had led his exiled people back to their land after Babylonian armies had destroyed Jerusalem. Like John, Salathiel calls Rome by the code name "Babylon," since the Romans, too, had destroyed Jerusalem; and, like John, he is careful to refer to Rome in language obscure to outsiders. No doubt Salathiel would have applauded how John, adopting Isaiah's image for ancient Tyre, pictured Rome as a once rich and proud queen, now beaten down and left bleeding in the dust like a common prostitute. Speaking as Ezra, Salathiel cries out to God, asking how he could allow the Romans to destroy his own people:

> You delivered the city into the hands of your enemies. Then I said in my heart, Are those who live in Babylon any better? . . . I have seen countless evil deeds . . . during these thirty years, and my heart failed me, for *I have seen how you tolerate those who sin, and have spared those who do evil, and have destroyed your own people . . . and have not shown to anyone how your way may be understood . . . what nation has kept your commandments so well [as Israel]?*[10]

"Ezra" says that his agitated and passionate prayers yielded visions; God sent the angel Uriel, who "answered and said to me, 'Your understanding has failed completely regarding this world; do you think that you can comprehend the way of the Most High?'" Ignoring the angel's implication that he is being arrogant, Ezra boldly answers, "Yes, my lord." Uriel then demands that Ezra solve three cosmic riddles, promising that when he succeeds, the angel will tell him what he wants to know: "He said to me, 'Go, weigh for me the weight of fire, or measure for me a measure of wind, or call back for me the day that has passed.'"[11]

Uriel's riddles echo the conclusion of the Book of Job, when the Lord speaks from a whirlwind, ironically demanding answers no human being could give:

> Where were you when I laid the foundation of the earth? Tell me, if you have understanding. Who determined its measurements—surely you know? . . .
> Who laid its cornerstone when the morning stars sang together, and all the heavenly beings shouted for joy? . . .
> Where is the path to where the light dwells, and where is the place of darkness? Surely you know, for you were born then, and you are very old! . . . Does the rain have a father? . . . Who has given birth to the frost from the heavens? . . . Who has the wisdom to number the clouds?[12]

Ezra's readers would know that questions like these had awed and shamed Job for having questioned God's ways, and had forced him to admit that "I spoke what I did not understand; things too wonderful for me, which I did not understand . . . therefore I despise myself, and repent in dust and ashes."[13] Ezra's readers, familiar with the conventions of such wisdom literature, would expect that he, like Job, would now confess that such matters were far beyond his understanding.

Instead, Ezra breaks with conventional piety and refuses to be silenced. When Uriel triumphantly delivers the stock angelic line ("You cannot understand the things with which you have grown up; how, then, can you understand the way of the Most High?"), Ezra utters a blunt and poignant cry of despair: "I fell on my face, and said to him, 'It would be better for us not to be here, than to come here and live without God, and suffer and not understand why.'"[14] When the angel replies that "those who live on earth can understand only what is on earth," Ezra protests that he is asking not about things in heaven but only about what human beings experience right here on earth:

> I beseech you, my lord, why have I been endowed with the power of understanding? *For I did not want to ask about heavenly things, but about those things which we experience every day* . . . why the people you loved have been given to godless tribes . . . and *why we pass from the world like insects, and our life is like a mist?*[15]

What Ezra hears next resonates more with John of Patmos than Job, for now the Lord speaks about the end-time and the coming of God's judgment:

> The world is moving quickly to its end. . . . The days are coming when those who live on earth shall be seized with great terror . . . when I shall draw near to visit the inhabitants of earth, when I shall require from those who do evil the penalty of their sin.

On that day, the Lord says, "the trumpet shall sound, and when all hear it, they shall suddenly be terrified"; yet those faithful to God "shall see my salvation, and the end of my world."[16]

Like John, Ezra hears that when Judgment Day comes, swift and harsh, the Lord will destroy Babylon—that is, Rome—and send "my son, the messiah"[17] (although, as we noted, Ezra does not regard Jesus of Nazareth as that messiah). When Ezra asks whether he will live long enough to see that day, the angel replies, "I was not sent to tell you about your own life, for I do not know."[18] Fearing that he might not live to see God's justice come, Ezra asks what happens "after death, as soon as every one of us yields up his soul?" Now Ezra, like John, hears that even after death, those who scorn God, hate his people, and ignore his law shall suffer "fire and torments, grieving and sad," while the righteous enter into the Paradise of delight to "see with great joy the glory of [God]."[19]

Waking from these visions, Ezra says, "my body shuddered violently, and my soul was so troubled that I fainted. But the angel who had come and talked with me held me, and strengthened me, and set me on my feet."[20] But when the angel reproaches him for daring to ask whether God loves human beings, Ezra speaks for everyone who has experienced heartbreak:

> I spoke [that way] because of my grief . . . every hour I suffer agonies of heart, while I strive to understand the way of the Most High. . . . For it would have been better for the dust not to have been born, so that the mind might not have been made from it. But now the mind grows with us, and therefore we are tormented, because we die, and we are conscious of it.[21]

Although many of Ezra's questions go unanswered, he tells how his grief and anger came to be resolved—not by theological argument but through a powerful experience of compassion. Ezra says that the Lord told him to

> go into a field of flowers . . . and eat only the flowers of the field; eat no meat and drink no wine, but eat only flowers, and pray to the Most High continually; then I will come and talk with you.[22]

When he goes into the field and stays there alone for seven days, eating only vegetables and drinking water, he sees a woman crying, "deeply grieved at heart," her clothes ripped, her head grimy with ashes as she mourns inconsolably the death of her son, her only child. After the friends who came to comfort her finally leave her to sleep, she tells Ezra, "I got up in the night and fled, and came to this field, and I intend to stay here and eat and drink nothing, grieving until I die." Startled by her desperation, Ezra says, "I dismissed the thoughts with which I had been engaged, and turned to her and sought to console her." To stop her from killing herself, he rebukes her and offers hope: "If you acknowledge God's decree to be just, you will receive your son back in due time"—presumably, in the "age to come," in eternity.[23]

Like John of Patmos, Ezra says that he began writing his revelation in anguish, since the horrors he had witnessed during the war with Rome had shattered his faith. Yet although *intellectually* he had refused to accept what he heard about divine justice, his narrative shows that somehow he had internalized it. The scholar Michael Stone suggests that the author here alludes to a powerful experience of conversion, having found that he could console others only *after* he had put aside some of his own grief, along with the questions that had preoccupied him.[24] When he turned to console a heartbroken woman, he found himself speaking of God's justice, and even God's love, discovering within himself resources of compassion that released some of his own bitterness. Suddenly, Ezra says, he saw the woman's face turn radiant and flash like lightning: "I was too frightened to approach her . . . then she suddenly uttered a loud and terrifying cry."[25] Aghast, he watched her vanish and then transform into a great city. He fell unconscious, and he says that when he came to, an angel helped him to stand and revealed that the grieving woman was actually his beloved Jerusalem, who, after being ravaged by the horrors of war and having mourned for her dead children, was transformed into the new and glorious city of Zion, which John, too, claimed to have seen.

Ezra's account of loss becomes, then, a vision that finally encompasses the devastation—and hope for healing—of a whole nation. The following night, he receives a terrifying vision of Rome, "the fourth kingdom which appeared in a vision to your brother Daniel." Drawing upon Daniel's prophecy, just as John had, Ezra sees Rome as a monstrous beast rising from the sea and as an enormous eagle with three heads, showing that this empire is "headed" by three rulers, apparently alluding to the three emperors who destroyed Jerusalem—Vespasian, Titus, and Domitian, the latter still reigning as he writes. Thus Ezra, like John, expresses anger over Israel's destruction and longs for God to set things right as he looks forward to the day when God's messiah casts Israel's oppressors into a fiery pit, raises the righteous back to life, and reigns in the new Jerusalem.

John of Patmos had ended his revelations there—in judgment,

fire, and glory—but Ezra turns from these, hoping for still more exalted inspiration. Imagining that the pagan nations had burned and destroyed Israel's Torah and Scriptures, the prophet asks the Holy Spirit to inspire him so that he might restore revelation to the human race. Following instructions he receives in a vision, he goes back to the field, this time bringing piles of writing tablets and five expert scribes:

> And on the next day, behold, a voice called to me, saying, "Ezra, open your mouth, and drink what I give you to drink." Then I opened my mouth, and behold a cup was offered to me, full of something like water . . . but its color was like fire. And I took it and drank; and when I had drunk it, my heart poured forth understanding, and wisdom increased in my breast, and my spirit retained its memory; and my mouth was opened.[26]

Seeing the spirit as divine intoxication, Ezra says that inspired words now poured forth from him, so that "during forty days, ninety-four books were written." The first twenty-four, he says, turned out to be the traditional twenty-four books of the Hebrew Scriptures, which the Lord told him to publish for everyone to read. But Ezra says that he was told to keep secret the *seventy* books that followed and show them to no one but "the wise," for "in them are the springs of understanding, the fountains of wisdom, and the river of knowledge."[27] Through this vision, Ezra boldly suggests that the whole Hebrew Bible, including the writings of Isaiah, Jeremiah, and Daniel that shaped John's Book of Revelation, and much of his own, amount to only a *small part* of all inspired sacred writings. Furthermore, he implies that such secret writings, although written long after the biblical ones, contain even more insightful revelations, among which he tacitly—and cleverly—includes the one he is now writing, the Revelation of Ezra itself.

Around 90 c.e., when Ezra was writing about two kinds of sacred books—open books and secret ones—many followers of Jesus, like John of Patmos, understood "the Scriptures" to mean, quite simply, the Hebrew Bible. Yet as more of Jesus' followers began to write books, their sacred collections, like Ezra's, came to include *both* kinds of writing—some open to everyone, like the New Testament gospels, and other books written and treated as secret writings (in Greek, *apocrypha*). Like Jews today who are familiar with the mystical teachings of kabbalah, Muslims who embrace Sufism, or Hindus or Buddhists who know Tantra, many Christians during those early centuries had heard not only of Jesus' *public* teaching from books like the gospels of Matthew and Luke but also of a wide range of *secret* gospels and revelations, like the Revelation of Peter, with which we began, and the Secret Revelation of John, which, like the Revelation of Ezra, was widely read in early Christian groups.[28] This Secret Revelation, attributed to Jesus' disciple John, whom many identified with John of Patmos, apparently was written to supplement what John of Patmos wrote.

The Secret Revelation of John opens in crisis as the disciple John, grieving Jesus' death, is walking toward the temple to worship when he meets a Pharisee who mocks him for having been deceived by a false messiah, these taunts echoing John's own fear and doubt. Devastated, John turns away from the temple and heads toward the desert, where, he says, "I grieved greatly in my heart." Suddenly, like John of Patmos before him, he says he saw brilliant light as the heavens opened, and the earth shook beneath his feet: "I was afraid, and then in the light I saw a child standing by me." Terrified, John says he saw there a luminous presence that kept changing form, and then heard Jesus' voice speaking from the light: "John, John, why do you doubt, and why are you afraid? . . . I am the one who is with you always. I am the Father; I am the Mother; I am the Son."[29]

The Jesus who appears in the Secret Revelation does not look as he does in John of Patmos' visions. Instead of a divine warrior leading heavenly armies to "strike down the nations," he appears here as the apostle Paul says he saw him—in blazing light and a heavenly voice, and then in changing forms, first as a child, then as an old man, then—and here scholars disagree—either as a servant or as a woman.[30] And while John of Patmos says that Jesus showed him "the things that are about to take place," the Jesus who appears in the Secret Revelation reveals not only future events but "what is visible and invisible"—what is already, and always, present.

Much of the Secret Revelation of John apparently draws upon esoteric—or, as some would say, mystical—Jewish tradition. As John continues to question "the Lord," he hears that God transcends anything we can understand: "it is infinite light." When John keeps asking "What can we know?" the divine voice explains that although God's transcendent being, characterized as masculine ("primordial Father"), is beyond human comprehension, what we *can* know of God is a genuine, but lesser, form of divine being, often characterized in feminine form, here called by various names—Protennoia (a Greek term that could be translated as "primordial consciousness"), Mother, even Mother-Father or Holy Spirit. [31]

Why, then, do so many people live ignorant of God, hopeless and despairing? John says that Christ answered with a creation story: when the divine Mother brought forth heavenly beings to rule over the heavens—sun, moon, and stars—these luminous powers conspired to dominate the human race. Since they hoped to obliterate awareness of the transcendent God and attract worship to themselves instead, they cast fear and desire "like nets" over human beings, so that nearly every culture mistakenly worships the sun, moon, and stars. Yet because God originally created humankind "in his image," the celestial powers failed to eradicate every trace of "the luminous *epinoia,*" that is, the capacity for spiritual insight, hidden deep within each one of us.

Hearing this, John takes heart: "I said, 'Christ, will everyone's soul live in the pure light?'" Jesus replies, "You have gained great insight.... Those on whom the Spirit of life will descend... will be saved... and purified... from all evil."[32] John keeps questioning: who will be saved? Does God's spirit come to everyone, or only to certain people? Jesus answers that salvation is available to *everyone,* since God's spirit is essential for life: "The power enters into every human being, for without [the spirit] they could not even stand upright."[33] The Secret Revelation concludes as Jesus says to John, "I have told you all these things so that you might write them down, and give them secretly to your kindred spirits, for this is the mystery of those who become spiritually stable."[34] Thus the Secret Revelation suggests that what is revealed to John is potentially available to all people, since all have received the same spirit—or, at least, to all who are receptive to what the spirit teaches.

The Secret Revelation (Apocryphon) of James, discovered in a volume found with others that contain copies of the Secret Revelation of John, says that James, Jesus' brother, copied this book in response to a request

> that I send you a secret book [in Greek, *apocryphon*] that was revealed to me and Peter by the Lord, and I could neither deter you nor deny what you ask; but I have written it in Hebrew, and have sent it to you, and to you alone.

James adds that "I sent to you, ten months ago, another secret book which the Savior had revealed to me." The author of the Secret Revelation, speaking as James, tells how the disciples, after Jesus' death, began to write down what they had heard him teach, some writing "open" books and others "secret" books, like this one:

> The twelve disciples were all sitting together and recalling what the Savior had said to each one of them, whether in secret or openly, and putting it into books.[35]

While the disciples were busy writing, James says, and "I was writing what was in my book," suddenly, to their astonishment, "the Savior appeared, having departed from us as we gazed after him." Here the author deliberately recalls—and challenges—what many Christians believe, having read the New Testament Book of Acts. For the Book of Acts says that after Jesus died, he appeared to his disciples in resurrected form and continued to speak with them *for forty days,* but that then he ascended bodily into heaven: "As they were watching . . . a cloud took him out of their sight. While he was going . . . they were gazing upward toward heaven."[36] Traditionally, Christians have taken this to mean that *after* that time, those seeking access to Jesus could find it only indirectly, through "apostolic tradition," as they called the oral and written accounts that the apostles were said to have handed down for the benefit of those born too late to ever speak directly with Jesus.

This Secret Revelation pictures "the twelve disciples" writing down what Jesus had told them, to hand down his teaching for later generations, as if they, too, believed that since Jesus had left them, direct access to him had ended. The author of the Secret Revelation of James challenges this assumption by setting the opening scene *a year and a half* after Jesus' death, saying that when the disciples suddenly saw Jesus standing among them, they reacted with shock. Instead of welcoming him with joy, at first they ask incredulous questions, as if he could not—or should not—be there: "And *five hundred and fifty days after he had risen from the dead,* we said to him, 'Have you departed, and removed yourself from us?'" To their surprise, Jesus says that he has neither left them behind nor ended their contact. "Jesus said, 'No; but I shall go to the place from whence I came. If you wish to come with me, come!'"[37] When they hesitate, Jesus urges them to take the initiative in speaking with him, then takes James and Peter aside, apparently because he finds them more receptive than the others, and offers to "fill" them.

Thus the Secret Revelation of James invites—and encourages— its hearers to seek ongoing revelation, then shows Jesus teaching them *how* to do so. For first Jesus tells Peter and James that it was not only during his earthly lifetime that he came to them; *even now* he comes to those open to receive him:

> I came down to dwell with you, so that you, in turn, might dwell with me. And finding your houses open to the heavens, I have come to dwell in the houses that could receive me at the time of my descent.[38]

Whoever is open to his presence, then, may learn how to engage in "dialogue with the risen Jesus." As a first step, Jesus urges them to seek to understand what he has already taught. Speaking with some impatience, he challenges James and Peter to recall the parables of "the seed," the "lamps of the virgins," the "wages of the workmen," and "the lost coin"—parables familiar from the gospels of Matthew and Luke. Jesus promises that when they actually understand what these parables mean, they will see that the kingdom of God is not just an event coming at the end-time but a reality into which one may enter here and now. But Jesus says that whoever wants to understand this must come to know God *experientially*, through an inner, intuitive kind of knowing: "unless you receive this through *gnosis*, you will not be able to find [the kingdom]." Next Jesus offers paradoxical teaching, urging Peter and James not only to *follow* him but even to "*become better than I; make yourselves like the son of the Holy Spirit!*"[39] As the Secret Revelation of James concludes, Jesus teaches them how to pray so that they may send heart, mind, and, finally, spirit into heaven. So, James says,

> we bent our knees, Peter and I, and gave thanks, and sent our hearts upward to heaven. We heard with our ears, and

saw with our eyes, the noise of wars, and a trumpet blast . . .
and when we had passed beyond that place, we sent our
minds farther upward, and saw and heard hymns and angelic blessing, and angels rejoicing . . . and we, too, rejoiced.

After this, we wanted to send our spirit upward to the
Majesty.[40]

Here the Secret Revelation of James apparently alludes to practices not spelled out in detail, traditions of spiritual ascent that, as
we shall see, various religious groups taught to their members.[41]

When scholars first read the Secret Revelation of John, the
Secret Revelation of James, and other books found at Nag Hammadi, we noticed that many—even most—include "dialogues"
with Jesus or with another divine revealer.[42] Several of us were
editing the Dialogue of the Savior—which consists of dialogue
between the risen Jesus and three close disciples, Matthew, Mary
Magdalene, and Judas—when our colleague and mentor, Professor Helmut Koester, asked a key question: "How would someone
have written this kind of dialogue?" As our work progressed, we
suggested that Christians then, like many today, struggling to
understand Jesus' teachings, imagined themselves as Jesus' earliest disciples. Some sought through prayer and meditation to
engage in "dialogue with the savior" as they questioned what certain sayings and parables meant. The Dialogue of the Savior suggests that they also engaged in discussion with one another,
perhaps recalling Jesus' saying that "where two or three are gathered together in my name, I am there among them."[43] When new
insights came to them, they would receive these as divine revelations and write them down, understanding what they had received

through prayer, reflection, and discussion as part of their ongoing "dialogue with the risen Jesus."

The Secret Revelation of James, the Secret Revelation of John, and the Dialogue of the Savior also show *how* to seek revelation. Each of these "revelations" includes prayer. The Secret Revelation of James is preceded by the Prayer of the Apostle Paul, a prayer that echoes Paul's words and asks for illumination:

> You are my mind; bring me forth! You are my treasury; open for me! You are my fulfillment; take me to you! ... Grant what no angel's eye has seen, and no ruler's ear has heard, and what has not entered into the human heart.[44]

Whoever opened the heavy leather-bound book called Codex I to begin devotions, then, would likely begin with this prayer and conclude with the praise that the scribe who copied it added at the end: "Christ is holy!" Other books also contain prayers to guide the reader, and some suggest specific techniques meant to help invoke revelation. The Dialogue of the Savior says that Jesus took his disciples to a remote place, where he placed his hands on their heads as he prayed "that they may see"[45] the path he opened up before them.

Around the same time that these texts were written, certain freelance Christian teachers apparently used techniques like these to invoke the Holy Spirit to come to their followers. The charismatic prophet Marcus, for example, who claimed to have received visions from God, preached around 160 c.e. in rural Gaul, encouraging his hearers to seek divine inspiration. When Marcus attracted large crowds from local Christian congregations, Irenaeus, the local bishop, charged that he was demon-possessed, a fraud and seducer. Irenaeus apparently had investigated Marcus' methods, for he derisively tells how, when someone came to Marcus requesting prayer, the prophet would place his hands on the person's head and invoke divine grace. Irenaeus claims even to know the actual prayer that he says Marcus offered, which echoes Jesus' parable of faith as a mustard seed:

> May Grace, who exists before the universe, and transcends all understanding and speech, fill your inner being, and multiply in you her own knowledge [in Greek, *gnosis*], sowing the mustard seed in you, as in good ground.[46]

Irenaeus also seems to have read the Secret Revelation of John, or similar "secret writings," since he briefly describes its content. He sharply warns his congregations to reject

> the unspeakable number of apocryphal and illegitimate writings, which [the heretics] themselves have forged, to confuse the minds of foolish people who are ignorant of the true Scriptures.[47]

Many "secret writings" recently discovered at Nag Hammadi in Egypt begin with prayer before encouraging their hearers to ask questions about Jesus' teachings and about the meanings of the Scriptures. In the Secret Revelation of John, for example, John asks Jesus about the account in Genesis 1—what happened "in the beginning," and what this says about the human condition. In the Dialogue of the Savior, Mary Magdalene asks Jesus about his parable of the mustard seed and about certain sayings—"Today's trouble is enough for today" (Matthew 6:34)—before she receives new insight and speaks "as a woman who had completely understood."[48] Thus in this dialogue she shows how a disciple, questioning Jesus in prayer, may come to deeper understanding. As we have seen, other texts, from the Revelation of Ezra to the Secret Revelation of James, also offer hints of ritual practices like baptism and specific disciplines of fasting and prayer intended to guide the heart, mind, and spirit and turn them toward God.

Each of these revelations shows its protagonist—whether Peter, Ezra, Mary Magdalene, Matthew, or James—undergoing spiritual transformation. Thus Ezra begins by telling how grief kept him awake night after night, "greatly aroused in my spirit, and my soul in distress," and concludes as he rises and walks through a field praising God, no longer pleading for help but having found consolation he hopes can help others. So, too, the Secret Revelation of James opens with James and the other disciples describing what they previously had heard from Jesus, unaware that he is still accessible, but ends as he and Peter bring new revelation to the other disciples. The Gospel of Truth, also found at Nag Hammadi, has a wider scope: it tells how all beings, alienated from God, suffer anguish and terror as they search "for the One from whom they came forth"[49] and ends as those who receive the true gospel are resting in God, no longer searching for truth, since "they themselves are the truth . . . and the Father is within them, and they are in the Father . . . set at rest, refreshed in the spirit."[50]

Although we do not know for sure who collected the "revelations" found at Nag Hammadi, many scholars think they were Christian monks who appreciated a wide range of disparate sources, perhaps including such non-Christian writings as the

Discourse on the Eighth and Ninth. This remarkable discourse recounts spiritual transformation through prayer and dialogue— but not with Jesus. Instead the discourse describes dialogue between a young Egyptian devotee of the Greek god Hermes and his spiritual teacher. Impatiently seeking enlightenment, the young man reminds his spiritual teacher that he has already worked through the required preliminaries, and now expects results: "O my father, yesterday you promised that you would bring my mind into the eighth, and afterwards into the ninth,"[51] that is, into the higher levels at which human consciousness may unite with the divine. Acknowledging that the initiate has struggled hard to purify his body, master his emotions, and discipline his mind by studying "the wisdom [found] in books," the teacher protests that he only can set forth "the order of the tradition." He cannot guarantee union with God. But the teacher tells his frustrated "son" to join with his spiritual brothers and "pray to God with all our mind, and all our heart and our soul, to ask him that the gift of the eighth extend to us."[52] The son prays intensely, while his spiritual father praises God in prayer that moves beyond intelligible words into divine names and mantras: "Zoxathazo a oo ee ooooooooooo . . . zozazoth." Telling his son to "sing a hymn in silence," the teacher enters into ecstatic union and embraces his disciple, exclaiming that he sees "the power, which is light, coming to us":

> I see! I see indescribable depths; how shall I tell you, my son? I am consciousness, and I see the consciousness that moves the soul! . . . You give me power! I see myself! I want to speak; fear restrains me. . . . I have seen! Language is not able to reveal this.[53]

Seeing his teacher transformed as he embodies the divine Hermes Trismegistus ("thrice greatest"), who mediates between heaven and earth, the initiate praises God and then begins to shout:

Father Trismegistus! What shall I say? We have received this light, and I myself see this same vision in you. . . . I am the instrument of your spirit; consciousness is your plectrum. . . . I see myself! I have received power from you, for your love has reached us. . . . I have received life from you. . . . I praise you; I call your name, hidden within me: a o ee o eee ooo iii oooo oooooo ooo oo uuuuu oo oooooooooooo.[54]

The book called Allogenes (Greek for "The Stranger") also relates dialogue between an initiate, Allogenes, and a spiritual teacher, this one more than human—a feminine angelic being whom he calls "all glorious Youel." Weaving Jewish esoteric lore associated with Adam and Eve's third son, Seth, often called "the stranger," together with Neoplatonic concepts of cosmology into teachings that also may include Buddhist meditation practices, the author of Allogenes sets out to show how to realize one's spiritual self.

Allogenes says that when Youel first spoke to him, "I fled and was very disturbed"; but that after "I turned to myself" and began to engage in intense meditation and "saw the light that surrounded me, and the good that was in me, I became divine."[55] Youel then begins to show him the structure of divine reality and promises that despite the difficult path ahead, "if you completely devote yourself to seeking, you shall know the good that is in you, and then . . . you shall know yourself as one who comes from the God who truly exists."[56] Allogenes says that "I did not despair of the words that I heard, but I prepared myself, and deliberated with myself for a hundred years."[57] After what seemed like endless time, Allogenes reports that he, like Ezekiel and Paul of Tarsus, was taken out of the body and received visions; yet this was only the beginning. Youel then taught him more:

> When you become afraid, withdraw back . . . and when you become complete where you are, still yourself. Do not desire to be active, lest you diminish your receptiveness to the Unknowable One.[58]

Practicing what she taught, Allogenes says he began to experience "within me a stillness of silence, and . . . I knew my true self . . . and I was filled with revelation by means of a primary revelation," apparently a firsthand experience of coming to know "the One who exists in me."[59] Allogenes concludes with a paradox: that the One he has come to know within himself cannot be known except through what Jewish and Christian mystics later called the *via negativa*, the way of "unknowing." Allogenes says he wrote this book for his own disciple, "full of joy . . . I wrote this book which was appointed for me, my son Messos, so that I might reveal to you what was proclaimed before me in my presence."[60]

These books of revelation have taken us a long way from the Revelation of John of Patmos—but the revelation called Thunder, Perfect Mind (more literally translated "Thunder, Complete Mind"[61]) takes us even further. For where John of Patmos sees only opposites—Christ against Satan, the saved and the damned, holiness and filth, the virgin bride and the whore of

Babylon—this revelation sees opposites in dynamic interaction and so claims to speak for the *complete* mind." Thunder was written as a poem to chant or a hymn to sing, in the voice of "thunder," heard in many cultures as a divine voice—from the Greeks, who called Zeus "the thunderer," to the God of Israel, often manifested in thunder, who, the Gospel of John says, spoke to Jesus as "a voice from heaven," which other bystanders heard only as thunder.[62]

Yet Thunder, Perfect Mind envisions thunder as a *feminine* power, perhaps because the Greek word for "thunder," *bronte*, is feminine—a power in whom all opposites meet:

> I was sent forth from the power,
>   and I have come to those who reflect upon me,
>   and I have been found among those who seek after me . . .
>
> Do not be ignorant of me at any time . . .
>
> For I am the first and the last.
> I am the honored one, and I am the scorned one.
> I am the whore and the holy one.
> I am the wife and the virgin.
> I am the mother and the daughter . . .
> I am the barren one,
>   and many are her children.
> I am she whose wedding is great,
>   and I have not taken a husband . . .
> I am the bride and the bridegroom,
>   and it is my husband who begot me.[63]

While the form of this poem resembles hymns to the Egyptian goddess Isis, several passages hint that the speaker also may be seen as Eve, "begotten," so to speak, from Adam. Since the divine voice speaks through human beings as well as divine ones, apparently this presence cannot be limited to a particular person, nor called by a single name. Instead the poem called Thunder, Perfect Mind, which contemporary American authors from Toni Morrison to Leslie Marmon Silko have woven into their writing, speaks as if the divine presence were everywhere—worshipped in Egypt as the goddesses Isis and Hathor but often ignored among "the barbarians," that is, among Jews and Christians who recognize no feminine deity. "Loved everywhere" for bringing forth life, she is also "hated everywhere" for bringing death, just as the Genesis story blames Eve, whose Hebrew name means "life," for bringing death:

> I am the one whose image is great in Egypt
>   and the one who has no image among the barbarians,
> I am the one who has been hated everywhere,
>   and who has been loved everywhere.
> I am the one whom they call Life,
>   and you have called Death . . .
> I am godless,
>   and I am one whose God is great.[64]

The poem praises a power manifested in both "the whore and the holy one," a presence found not only in palaces but also where one least expects it: "cast out upon the dung heap . . . among those who are disgraced . . . among those violently slain." The voice claims to speak through

the spirits of every man who lives with me,
and of women who dwell within me . . .
I am she who cries out . . .
I prepare the bread, and the mind within.
I am the knowledge of my name.[65]

Whoever recognizes that voice, the poem concludes, will recognize his or her own name in relationship to that divine energy.

While John of Patmos acknowledges no feminine power within the divine, many of the "revelations" found at Nag Hammadi, from the Secret Revelation of John to Allogenes and Thunder, Perfect Mind, give voice to feminine manifestations of God. According to the revelation called the Trimorphic Protennoia (Greek for "The Triple-Formed Primordial Consciousness"), the voice who says she existed before creation and "moves in every creature" speaks of how all beings intuitively long to commune with her, God's immanent presence:

I move in every creature . . . in everyone, and I delve into
them all. . . . I am a voice speaking softly. . . . I dwell in the
silence. . . . I am perception, and knowing [*gnosis*]. . . . *I am
the real voice. I cry out in everyone, and they recognize me,
since a seed indwells them. . . . I am the awareness of the
Father . . . a hidden thought . . . a mystery.*[66]

The Trimorphic Protennoia recalls the opening of the Gospel of John, which tells how "in the beginning," God became manifest in *masculine form, as divine word,* and declares that God had previously become manifest in feminine form, as divine *voice.* Though this interior voice is so often drowned out by other noise, the Trimorphic Protennoia says that it speaks "in every creature," to all people everywhere. Whoever wrote this revelation was probably familiar with Jewish traditions that, as noted above, envision God's immanent aspect as feminine, manifested as "spirit" (*ruah*), "wisdom" (*hokmah*), or "presence" (*shekinah*).

What are we to make of this outpouring of books of revelation—Jewish, Christian, pagan—during those early centuries? And why was John of Patmos' very different book the *only* "book of revelation" included in the New Testament? Some scholars who study the Nag Hammadi texts have said that such writings deserved to be excluded, because they appeal to a spiritual elite. There may be truth in this, for unlike John of Patmos' hugely popular revelations, which he probably intended to have read, or preached, in public worship,[67] these secret writings tend to prescribe arduous prayer, study, and spiritual discipline, like Jewish mystical texts and esoteric Buddhist teachings, for those engaged in spiritual quest.

Although it's difficult to generalize about such diverse "other revelations," many do differ markedly from John's also in the way they envision the relationship between humankind and God. Most Jews, Christians, and Muslims avoid characterizing their relationship with God as do the initiates in Allogenes and the "Discourse," who seek to discover themselves within the divine. Orthodox adherents of monotheistic traditions draw clear boundaries between themselves and God. The Jewish theologian Martin Buber could speak to God as "I *and* Thou," as a relationship between creature and creator, but he could *not* have said, "I *am*

Thou," as a devout Hindu might say, "Thou art *that*," collapsing the boundaries that separate human from divine.

Yet as we've seen, many of the sources found at Nag Hammadi do encourage spiritual seekers to seek union with God, or to identify with Christ in ways that fourth-century "orthodox" Christians would censor. In the Gospel of Mary Magdalene, for example, Mary encourages her fearful fellow disciples by saying, "The Son of Man is within you; follow him!" The author of *The Teachings of Silvanus*, alluding to images of Christ as "the way" and "the door," suggests that one may find access to God through one's own spiritual self:

> Knock upon *yourself* as upon a door, and walk upon *yourself* as on a straight road. For if you walk on the road, you cannot get lost.... Open the door for yourself, that you may know the One who is.... What you open for yourself, you will open.[68]

The Gospel of Philip, too, urges believers to become "no longer a Christian, but a Christ!"[69] And since such writings are directed toward people willing to devote themselves to spiritual practice and seek direct contact with God, they tend to bypass any need for "clergy."

During the fourth century, bishops who followed Irenaeus, intent on establishing "orthodoxy," would work hard to suppress writings like these. Although such bishops did not deny that Jesus was human, they tended to place Jesus on the divine side of the equation—not only divine but, in the words of the Nicene Creed, which they would soon endorse, "God from God . . . *essentially the same as God*."[70] Orthodox theologians insisted that the rest of humankind, apart from him, are only transitory creatures, lost in sin—a view that would support what would become their dominant teaching about salvation, offered only through Christ, and, in particular, through the church they claimed to represent.

In the meantime, there was trouble. From the late second century, Christian leaders, who saw their close groups torn apart internally as Roman magistrates arrested and executed their most outspoken members, felt that John's Book of Revelation spoke directly to these crises—and so they championed John of Patmos' book above all others and defended it, as we shall see, against its critics, both pagan and Christian.

CHAPTER FOUR

Confronting Persecution:
How Jews and Christians Separated
Politics from Religion

Seventy years after John wrote Revelation, his visions of terror and hope inspired a revival movement called the New
Prophecy—an early instance of how John's prophecies have galva-
nized Christians to this day. Earthquakes, plague, and outbreaks
of violence convinced the "new prophets"—as they have persuaded
countless others throughout two thousand years—that they were
living in the last days before God's final judgment.

The revival began in the late 160s, when a Christian named
Montanus began speaking "in the spirit" near Philadelphia, a city
in Asia Minor famous for its prophets, where, Montanus liked to
point out, the Son of Man first revealed to John of Patmos an
"open door" into heaven. Nearby, only a few years later, a woman
follower of Montanus named Quintilla received a vision of Christ
descending to her—this time in the form of a woman—to reveal
that the "new Jerusalem" John had foreseen was about to descend,
spelling Rome's downfall.[1]

When the African convert Tertullian heard Montanus' followers testify how the Holy Spirit had come upon them, he was
amazed to learn how this charismatic movement inspired by
John's prophecy had swept through the empire, from John's territory in Asia Minor to Rome, and then to provinces as remote as

Gaul and Africa, where "it gained its greatest success."[2] Everywhere Montanus traveled with the two women prophets who initiated the revival with him, Priscilla and Maximilla, they aroused enthusiastic supporters—and hostile opponents. Those who accused the "new prophets" of being inspired by Satan also attacked John's now famous—or infamous—Book of Revelation, saying that what it "revealed" was nothing but the mad ravings of a heretic. Since the time of John's writing, however, much had changed. While he had addressed small groups of Jesus' followers living precariously on the margins of the great cities of Asia Minor, Tertullian, writing more than seventy years later from the prosperous African port city of Carthage, boasted that Christians

emerged only yesterday, and we have filled every place among you—cities, islands, fortresses, towns, market-places, the army itself, tribes, companies, the imperial palace, the Senate, the Forum—we have left nothing to you but the temples of your gods![3]

What delighted Tertullian alarmed Roman magistrates. A movement that they had regarded as a marginal nuisance was becoming a cause for serious concern as groups now organized and headed by bishops attracted many new converts, especially among the urban poor.[4] Yet citizens loyal to Rome, shocked by recent disasters—huge earthquakes and a terrifying outbreak of plague—suspected that the gods were angry, most likely at the growing number of "atheists" (Christians) being tolerated within their domain. By 180 c.e. the authorities had stepped up arrests of known leaders. Tertullian says that in Carthage, soldiers would burst into private homes to break up meetings of Christians gathered to worship.[5] Even though they seized only a few people, their tactics terrified many more. News of those arrested and killed traveled fast through Christian groups worldwide and heightened the fears of those who survived.

During these desperate times, the prophet Montanus urged his fellow believers to stand with him as he echoed the prophecies of Isaiah and John of Patmos, warning that the present turmoil portended the "day of vengeance" when God would shatter and transform the world. Like the classical prophets, Montanus proclaimed what he said "the Lord has spoken":

> I am about to create new heavens and a new earth. . . . I am about to create Jerusalem as a joy, and its people as a delight . . . no more shall the sound of weeping be heard in it, or the cry of distress. . . . The wolf and the lamb shall feed together, the lion shall eat straw like the ox. . . . They shall not hurt or destroy on all my holy mountain, says the Lord.[6]

Because Montanus often claimed to speak in God's name, saying, for example, "neither an angel nor a messenger, but I, the Lord God, the Father, have come,"[7] hostile listeners swore that he thought he was God—or at least the Holy Spirit—in person. Montanus objected that, like prophets before him, from Isaiah and Ezekiel to John of Patmos, he had been caught up "in the spirit" so that God might speak through him. He used prophetic language, he said, because a human being can become God's instrument only when ordinary consciousness is suspended:

Behold, the human being is like a lyre, and I alight like a
plectrum; the human being sleeps and I awaken; behold, it
is the Lord who changes human hearts, and gives a heart to
the people.[8]

When the movement began, Montanus, Priscilla, and Maximilla,
called the Three, had traveled from church to church in Asia
Minor, echoing John of Patmos' words as they proclaimed that
the Holy Spirit had come upon them to renew devotion to Christ
and to recall believers to "the love you had at first."[9] Both women,
testifying that they had been seized by the Holy Spirit, had left
their husbands to travel with Montanus. Visits from the Three
attracted huge crowds all over the province. The boldness—and,
no doubt, the success—of their preaching inflamed their opponents, who called them demon-possessed and accused them of
disrupting worship as they prophesied in ecstatic trance, often
stirring audiences into frenzy. When angry church leaders ordered
Maximilla to be silent, she said that she could not obey them,
since she spoke not for herself but for Christ. "Do not listen to
me—listen to Christ!"[10] she declared when church officials seized
her to exorcise the devil from her. Her supporters fought them
off, but soon afterward a group of Asian bishops voted to excom-
municate her. Maximilla cried out that they had failed to recognize the Holy Spirit speaking among them: "I am driven away
from the sheep like a wolf. I am not a wolf; I am word, and spirit,
and power!"[11]

Heated arguments split churches throughout Asia Minor, threatening schism. A majority of bishops there voted to censor the "new
prophets" and declared that their two favorite books—the Book of

Revelation and the Gospel of John—contained nothing but blasphemous lies. Opponents of the New Prophecy appealed for support to the Christian bishop of Rome and found an advocate among his clergy. A Roman priest named Gaius challenged the new prophets and publicly argued that the books on which they relied for support, Revelation and John, both had been written not by a disciple but by a heretic named Cerinthus. Gaius insisted that the "age of prophecy" was over, having been succeeded by the "age of the apostles," now represented by clergy like himself.

Other Christians disagreed. In Rome, the convert Justin, called the Philosopher, seized on the Book of Revelation during a debate with the Jewish philosopher Trypho as proof that "the gifts of prophecy, which previously resided among your people, have now been transferred to us"[12]—that is, to Christians. Perhaps to silence critics like Gaius, Justin insisted that the Book of Revelation was not heretical but had been written when "a man among us named John, one of Christ's disciples, received a revelation."[13] Justin was the first, so far as we know, to claim that John of Patmos was none other than *John of Zebedee,* Jesus' actual disciple.

What made the Book of Revelation especially compelling to Justin were events he was seeing before his own eyes around the years 160 to 165—events that he believed John had prophesied. Justin declared that John, like Jesus, had "predicted that we would be slaughtered and hated for the sake of his name . . . and this has actually happened."[14] Justin was distressed to hear that the city prefect had arbitrarily killed a Christian philosopher named Ptolemy, and he says he knew of "similar things being done everywhere by the governors."[15] Fearful of persecution, Justin agreed with John of Patmos that demonic powers were inciting Rome's rulers to hunt and kill Christians.[16] He echoed John's warning that Satan attacks God's people on two fronts at once: externally, through Roman authorities, and internally, through heretics who corrupt Christian groups from within.

Justin dared write an open letter to the emperor Antoninus Pius and his sons, Marcus Aurelius and Lucius Verus, protesting persecution and pleading with them to stop the killings. Justin addresses these rulers as fellow philosophers, asking them to listen to reason and arguing that Christians are model citizens. Then, however, he turns to threats that the emperors would have ridiculed. Invoking John's prophecy, he warns them that "if you pay no attention to our pleas and clear explanations," soon they will suffer "punishment in eternal fire," when Jesus returns from heaven in glory as warrior and judge to reign over the world from Jerusalem. Justin adds that

> if you read these words in a hostile spirit, you can do no more . . . than kill us, which indeed does no harm to us, but to you, and all who unjustly are enemies, and do not repent, brings eternal punishment by fire.[17]

Yet because Justin still hoped to find a way for people like himself to live peaceably under imperial rule, he sometimes changed his tone and addressed the emperors with cautious respect. What he wanted to do, after all, was revolutionary. In a world in which patriotism, family piety, and religious devotion were inseparable, Justin boldly tried to drive a wedge between what we call *politics* and *religion*—and so to create the possibility of a *secular* relationship to government. To persuade the emperors that this would not endanger the empire, he points out that Christians pay taxes and obey the laws; "more than all other people, we are your helpers and allies in promoting peace,"[18] and "we willingly serve you as human rulers,"[19] even though, he explains, Christians stop short of offering religious devotion to the gods, whom they see as "evil demons."

Justin knew that there was some precedent for what he was asking, especially since the emperor Augustus, around 6 C.E.,[20] had allowed Jews to demonstrate loyalty to Rome in ways that did not directly violate their ancestral customs. Augustus apparently had decided that forcing Jews to offer sacrifice to Rome's gods, as subject people routinely did, was more trouble than it was worth. So he ordered the Jews instead to pay special taxes and to sacrifice two lambs and a bull every day in their temple in Jerusalem and to offer these with prayers to *their* god for the emperor's welfare. By charging the cost of these sacrifices to his treasury, Augustus made a show of imperial generosity while forcing Jewish leaders to acknowledge his power in the heart of their own sanctuary. Accepting these terms allowed Jews to save face and survive; thus the Jewish historian Josephus wrote that sacrifices financed by the imperial treasury showed the emperor's respect for their nation and its god.[21]

Augustus' pragmatic strategy had set the terms under which Roman rulers and their Jewish subjects would contend for generations. But in 31 C.E., the emperor Gaius, often called by his childhood nickname Caligula ("Little Boots"), was rumored to have insisted on being worshipped as a god himself.[22] Philo, who led a delegation of Alexandrian Jews to meet with Gaius, reported that the emperor had complained to his delegation about Augustus' policy, saying that "you *did* sacrifice—but *to* another, even if it was *for* me. What good is it, then? For it wasn't *to* me."[23] After Caligula's assassination, many Romans regarded him as a "mad emperor," and his successors tended to revive Augustus' solution. Even in an empire in which *politics* and *religion* seemed inextricably intertwined, then, some Jews found ways to untwist these strands and open the way for what later generations would call separation of church and state.

Justin might have hesitated, however, to invoke Jews as an example of how people might withhold religious allegiance and still live as peaceable citizens, because Jews not only had started a war against Rome from 66 to 70 but had rebelled again, fighting a second Jewish war, from 115 to 117. Even worse, shortly before Justin petitioned the emperors, Jewish religious militants had ignited a *third* rebellion against Rome in 131—a four-year war that would be fresh in the minds of magistrates charged with keeping the peace. Roman officials who had heard of Jesus of Nazareth apparently regarded him as one of those religious militants and knew that many of his followers, like John of Patmos, hated Rome. As we've seen, Gentile converts like Justin might have aroused even more suspicion than Jews, since they had no ancestral tradition to blame for refusing to offer the ordinary tokens of loyalty to Rome. On June 1, 165, Justin was arrested, along with six of his students, and charged with being Christian. Rusticus, the city prefect, ordered Justin and his students to sacrifice to the gods. When they refused, Rusticus immediately sentenced them to be whipped and beheaded "in accordance with the laws."[24]

News of Justin's death traveled fast among Christian groups, along with several versions of the courageous way he had answered

Rusticus' interrogation at his trial. Such events offered fresh evidence to like-minded believers that John of Patmos was right: they were living through the sufferings of the end-time. Irenaeus, the Greek-speaking missionary from Asia Minor who had denounced Marcus in rural Gaul, probably never met Justin, but he respected his witness and agreed with him that John of Patmos' prophecies were divinely inspired.

Although, as we have noted, Irenaeus had denounced many *other* books that he called "illegitimate secret writings" (*apocrypha*), he championed John of Patmos' Book of Revelation. For as persecution intensified, Irenaeus, like Justin, believed that he was seeing John's prophecies of the end fulfilled before his eyes. Within a few years of Justin's death, Irenaeus would have been shocked to hear of at least twelve other Christians killed in his home city, Smyrna—and worst of all, that his beloved eighty-six-year-old mentor, Bishop Polycarp, had been hunted down, charged with being a Christian, and burned alive before shouting crowds in the city's sports arena. About ten years later, in 177, Irenaeus saw riots break out even in Gaul as believers were hounded and beaten and others arrested, imprisoned, tortured, and strangled, while, some said, more than forty "confessors," many of them known to him, were tortured and killed by wild animals in a public spectacle. Those who witnessed what happened on that summer day in 177 later wrote that although they could not begin to describe "the intensity of our afflictions here, the hatred of the pagans, and the magnitude of the martyrs' suffering,"[25] they recognized all these as the work of "the wild beast" that John of Patmos had predicted in "the Scriptures," among which they now included John's Book of Revelation.[26]

Irenaeus agreed. As he sought to restore the shattered congregations of Christians in Gaul after the killings of 177, he challenged those who dismissed the Book of Revelation as heresy, as the Roman priest Gaius had done. On the contrary, he declared, "the prophetic spirit" speaks through the Book of Revelation, and also through the Gospel of John. Those who reject these inspired books, he wrote, "disregard the gift of the spirit, which in these last days has been poured out upon the human race," and also will have to reject the apostle Paul, "since he speaks explicitly about prophetic gifts and recognizes both men and women prophesying."[27] Like Justin, Irenaeus endorsed the view that "John, the Lord's disciple" wrote both the Book of Revelation and the Gospel of John.

Critical readers from his time to the present have challenged this claim, pointing out that the two books diverge sharply in language and style. Yet identifying John of Patmos with Jesus' disciple helped domesticate this controversial prophet by drawing him into the circle of "the Twelve" and thus into ecclesiastically sanctioned authority. This identification served to bolster the claim that *both* controversial books go back to Jesus' earliest apostles, and so convey "apostolic" tradition. Thus the tradition that many people accept to this day—that Jesus' disciple John of Zebedee wrote both books—can be traced to Asia Minor during the mid-second century. Christians like Justin and Irenaeus championed this tradition, apparently to refute the charge that the heretic named Cerinthus had written both books. Irenaeus countered that rumor with a story he had heard older Christians tell, to show that John actually despised Cerinthus: one day, when John went to the public baths in Ephesus, he saw Cerinthus inside and rushed out without bathing, shouting to his companions, "Let's get out of here, lest the bath house fall down, because Cerinthus, the enemy of truth, is inside!"[28]

Irenaeus suggests that the increased intensity of persecution not only proves that John of Patmos' prophecies are true but also shows clear continuity between his prophecies and those of Daniel and Jesus. "What Daniel prophesied about the end-times has been confirmed by the Lord" when Jesus prophesied the desecration of the Jerusalem Temple, just as John, "writing at the time of Domitian, . . . has shown in the Revelation even more clearly what shall happen in the end-times."[29] Irenaeus declares that all three— Daniel, Jesus, and John of Patmos—anticipated "what shall happen in the time of Antichrist."[30] By linking John's visions of "the beast" and the "false prophet" with Antichrist, Irenaeus introduced an interpretation that, from his time to our own, has proved enormously influential. For although many readers, like Irenaeus, claim to find "the Antichrist"—that is, a false, deceptive messiah— in the Book of Revelation, this figure is never mentioned there. In all the New Testament, it is mentioned only in a short letter attributed to John,[31] although Irenaeus encouraged believers to see it implied as well in Daniel's vision of the "fourth beast"[32] and in the Gospel of John, where Jesus prophesies the coming of a "deceiver."[33]

By linking "the beast" with "Antichrist"—namely, that "the beast" who embodies *alien ruling powers* is also inextricably linked with *false belief,* and *false belief,* in turn, with *moral depravity*— Irenaeus makes a crucial interpretation of John's prophecies. Irenaeus wants to show that God's judgment demands not only *right action* but also *right belief.* At the same time, he wants to refute those who say that divine revelation comes to all people universally— a message that we have seen in many other "revelations." Irenaeus does concede that, "indeed, the coming of the Son is available to all people alike," but, he insists, "it is for the purpose of judgment, to separate the *believing* from the *unbelieving*." Lest anyone object that God judges not on the basis of what people *believe* but on the basis of what they *do*—whether they feed the hungry, clothe the destitute, and care for the sick and prisoners, as Jesus' parable of judgment says (Matthew 25:31ff)—Irenaeus insists that *moral action* and *right belief* are inseparable. He argues that only those who accept "true doctrine" actually *do* act morally; and from this he concludes that God's judgment will divide believers from non-believers.[34]

Because Irenaeus believes that in the persecutions he can see "the beast" at work, he finds John's visions of the end-time powerfully compelling. Like Justin, he also claims that "the beast" works not only through outsiders who persecute Christians but also through Christian insiders, the "false brethren" whom he calls *heretics*. Irenaeus draws upon the Book of Revelation to conclude his famous book *Against Heresies* with a dramatic picture of the last judgment—Christ returning from heaven in glory to fight and conquer "the beast," dividing the saved from the damned, then casting the beast and all his human followers down into the lake of fire to suffer eternal torment. Insisting that moral depravity is inseparably linked to false belief, Irenaeus ends his book by solemnly pronouncing God's judgment against Christians who *secretly* follow Satan, those internal enemies he calls *heretics*:

> Let those, therefore, who blaspheme the Creator, whether openly, or [covertly], . . . be recognized as agents of Satan by all who worship God—those through whose agency

Satan now has been seen to speak against God, who has prepared eternal fire for every kind of apostasy.[35]

Next Irenaeus turns to the external enemies, those who worship "the beast" who even now rules the world with his host of demonic spirits, deceiving, dominating, and terrorizing all nations, he says, as the power of evil has done for six thousand years. Irenaeus is fascinated by the mystery of the beast's identity, which for him holds the secret of the suffering he has seen. What is the meaning of the beast's "human number"? Who is he? When and how will his power be broken, his atrocities punished, and when will those he killed be raised back to life, their sufferings avenged?

Irenaeus knows, of course, that Rome is the empire that embodies "the beast," but he mentions it with great reticence, perhaps fearing reprisals. After saying that "all the most approved and ancient copies" of John's manuscript, as well as "those men who saw John face to face," agree that the beast's "human number," computed mathematically according to the numerical value assigned to each letter, is, indeed, 666, he acknowledges that "many names can be found possessing the number mentioned."[36] Cautiously saying that he still regards the question as unsolved, he mentions the Greek word *Lateinos*—"Latin"—which he says computes to 666, and offers this as "a very probable solution, since it is the name of the last of the four kingdoms seen by Daniel; *for the Latins are those who rule right now.*" Abruptly, then, as if fearing that he already has said too much, he hedges:

We will not, however, run the risk of pronouncing clearly the name of the Antichrist; for if it were necessary to reveal it at the present time, it would have been announced by him who had seen the revelation.[37]

While Justin and Irenaeus experienced the decades between 160 and 180 C.E. as the onslaught of the beast's persecution, many of their contemporaries saw these same years as the empire's golden age, when the "philosopher emperor," Marcus Aurelius, ruled Rome. Yet although Marcus was famous for integrity and fairness, he had no tolerance for Christians. He could see that sporadic reprisals had failed to check the Christian movement ever since 112 C.E., when Pliny, who governed Asia Minor, had written to the emperor Trajan to warn that this "dangerous infection" was spreading among people "of all ages and every rank, and also of both sexes."[38] Pliny reported that he didn't think that Christians actually ate human flesh in their rituals, as rumor held, but he did warn that their growing movement had coincided with a sharp decrease in government revenues from sacrificial meat, not only in the cities but also in rural areas. Pliny added that he thought there was still time to stamp it out and outlined the measures he had taken. As we have seen, he had released the accused who denied being Christians and who proved it by offering sacrifice to the gods or the emperor's statue and cursing Christ; those who refused he had sent to be killed immediately.

By the time Marcus Aurelius became emperor in 161, he and his advisers had begun to take Christians seriously as a threat. Around 165 C.E., M. Cornelius Fronto, an African orator who had risen to great prominence in Rome and was Marcus' teacher, close friend, and senior adviser, gave a widely publicized speech characterizing Christians as criminally minded people whose meetings were covers for secret rituals involving "people of both sexes, and all ages," including children, in group orgies:

> After feasting, when the banquet has warmed up and a passion for incestuous lust and drunkenness has flared up, a dog tied to the lamp is incited to jump and leap by throwing a little cake to it beyond the reach of the leash.[39]

Once the lights are out, Fronto went on, the guests fall upon one another in unrestrained orgies.

Marcus might have heard, too, from another close friend, Rusticus, his former philosophy teacher and now prefect of Rome, of a recent case in which he had interrogated seven accused Christians led by Justin—the same one who had petitioned Marcus—who called himself a "Christian philosopher." Surprised that all seven adamantly refused to offer sacrifice, even when facing the death sentence, Rusticus had asked, "If you are whipped and beheaded, do you believe that you will go up to heaven?" Justin had replied, "Not only do I *think* it; I am absolutely certain."[40] Rusticus might have reported how he then lost patience, gave them a final warning, and, when they spurned it, immediately ordered his soldiers to whip them and cut off their heads. Stories like this led Galen, Marcus' personal physician, to grudgingly admire the courage he had seen some of them show, although he thought they were fools to believe in miracles and dead people raised. Marcus himself, less forgiving of those accused of atheism and disloyalty to Rome, noted in his private journal that what some admired as courage was nothing but theatrical bravado.

When increasing pressure and more frequent arrests failed to stop the movement from growing, another member of Marcus' circle, the Platonic philosopher Celsus, wrote a serious critique to expose it.[41] Celsus might have intended to answer the two manifestos that Justin had written and published before his execution,[42] for he carefully investigated Christians and read their writings extensively. In his hugely influential attack, *The True Doctrine*, Celsus wrote that what alarmed him most was the sense of a hostile, breakaway faction forming—and growing dangerously—within the empire. Since Celsus devoutly worshipped the gods and supported the emperors, he despised Christians for aiming their message at disaffected and marginal people, appealing primarily to slaves, gullible women and children, pickpockets, thieves, and prostitutes. Yet who else, he asked, would believe their bizarre stories about the crucified Jew whom they worship as God? Who else would listen to the "terrors they invent" to scare people into believing, when they say that "God will come down and bring fire like a torturer"[43] to judge and punish everyone who rejects their teaching? Above all, Celsus ridiculed their threats of divine judgment:

> They are foolish, too, to imagine that when God applies the fire—like a cook!—all the rest of mankind will be thoroughly roasted, and that they alone will survive, not merely those who are alive at the time, but also those long dead who will rise up from the earth having the same bodies as before.[44]

Celsus accuses them of having joined a "secret society" and cut themselves off from the rest of civilization, acting as if "outsiders are not to be trusted, and that they themselves must remain perpetual apostates from the approved religions." Finally, he warns that if everyone were to adopt the Christians' attitude, there would be no rule of law; legitimate authority would be abandoned.[45]

Christians who defended the movement from such attacks sometimes confirmed the worst fears of critics like Celsus. Tertullian, the African convert, outraged when he saw Christians being killed in the sports arena in his home city of Carthage, praised "our own John" for picturing Rome as Babylon, "proud of her power, and victorious over the saints,"[46] but damned and doomed. Tertullian marveled at God's power made visible to thousands of spectators in Carthage on an unforgettable spring day, March 7, 203, when the twenty-two-year-old convert Perpetua walked steadily, with focused gaze, into the amphitheater to die for refusing to sacrifice to Rome and her gods.[47] While the crowd shouted and jeered, Perpetua and her doomed companions, Saturus and Saturninus, infuriated them even more by defiantly signaling, "You condemn us today; tomorrow God will condemn you!"[48]

While in prison, Perpetua wrote in her diary dreams that came to her—dreams infused with imagery from John's Book of Revelation. In one, she faced an enormous and terrifying dragon and dared step on its head as she climbed a ladder toward heaven; in another, she saw herself in the arena, having turned into a man, fighting in single-handed combat with the devil.[49] Whoever wrote the introduction to Perpetua's prison diary—and many believe that it was Tertullian—declared that the visions she received in prison, the healings she performed, and her courageous martyrdom along with her companions proved that the spirit of God was upon them, as it was upon the "new prophets," Montanus and his followers, whom the martyrs had admired. Who, having witnessed the superhuman courage that even Perpetua's slave Felicitas, along with Saturus and Saturninus, displayed during these ordeals could deny the martyrs' conviction that the Holy Spirit was shining through them?

Shortly after these executions, Tertullian himself joined the New Prophecy movement, inspired by John's Revelation, which had given courage to Perpetua and her companions throughout their ordeal. Tertullian, like Justin and Irenaeus, championed the writings that these martyrs especially loved—the Gospel of John and the Book of Revelation. Tertullian wrote for insiders that what spectators saw in the sports arena could not compare with the great spectacle he could hardly wait to see:

> What a spectacle is that fast-approaching coming of our Lord . . . now in triumph! What the kingdom of the righteous! What the city New Jerusalem! . . . What gives me joy? What arouses me to exaltation?
>
> I see so many brilliant rulers, whose ascension into the heavens was publicly proclaimed, now groaning in the lowest darkness . . . governors of provinces, too, who persecuted the Christian name, now in fires fiercer than those which they raged against Christ's followers! . . . I shall have a better chance to look on the chariot racers, glowing in their chariots of fire, and seeing the wrestlers, not in their gymnasia, but tossing in the fiery flames![50]

Writing his own impassioned defense of the Christians, *The Apology*, Tertullian expresses fierce ambivalence toward the empire.

Like Justin, at first he insists that Christians are the empire's best and most loyal subjects:

> We pray for all the emperors; we pray for long life; for the empire's security; for protection for the imperial household; for brave armies, a faithful senate, the world at peace—whatever, as a man or Caesar, an emperor could wish.[51]

But after defiantly adding that Christians pay taxes only because Jesus told them to do so[52] and that they subject themselves to "the powers that be" because Jesus' apostle Paul had told them that "all powers that exist are ordained by God for your good,"[53] Tertullian, like Justin, turns to threats. He warns that "there is another and greater necessity for us to pray for the emperors and for the complete stability of the empire," since "we know that a powerful shock impends over the whole earth—the final end of all things, threatening terrible sufferings"—horrors that have been delayed only because "we [Christians] pray for the delay of the final end."[54]

Defending "the new Christian society" as a model community,[55] Tertullian asks, if Roman magistrates allow subject nations to worship their own gods, why not allow Christians to do the same? Since Roman magistrates tolerate all kinds of foreign cults—Egyptian, Greek, and Persian—why not the cult of Christ? Tertullian would surely have known the answer to this preposterous suggestion, having risked his life to join the Christians, while cosmopolitan Roman citizens, even emperors, joined multiple cults with impunity.

How, then, did joining Christianity differ from joining any other religious group? To answer this question, let's consider what was written by another member of Marcus' circle, the brilliant and adventurous African philosopher Apuleius, a disciple of Plato fascinated by religion and magic, who made a practice of joining exotic cults. Like Justin and Tertullian, Apuleius was a spiritual seeker, who wrote that as a young man, "moved by religious fervor and passion to know the truth," he investigated religious groups of all kinds: "I was initiated into various Greek mysteries . . . and learned mysteries of many kinds, many rituals and diverse ceremonies."[56] Although sworn to not reveal the secrets of what happened in such initiations, he became famous for speaking in public about "how many mysteries I knew," including those of the Roman god Liber; the Persian god Mithra; the Greek god of healing, Asclepius; and his favorite, the Egyptian goddess Isis.

Apuleius wrote the only firsthand account we have of initiation into Isis' mysteries, but instead of a straightforward report, he offered the kind of dramatic, witty, and moving story his contemporaries had come to expect from a man whose private life had turned into a public spectacle in a packed courtroom. We know only his side of the story, which he told in court. He had been accused of practicing criminal magic after he induced a lonely widow, perhaps twice his age and enormously wealthy, to marry him and sign over her entire fortune to him. When the widow's son, formerly his friend and fellow student, furiously pressed charges, then suddenly died during the trial, his uncle immediately accused Apuleius of using magic—or poison—to murder the young man whom he had cheated of his inheritance.

At his trial, Apuleius scoffed at charges that he was a man of great vanity who kept his hair carefully coiffed and wrote erotic poetry to young boys, and that after he arrived in the city, relatively poor, and met the widow, witnesses had seen him buying special ingredients to make aphrodisiacs and performing magic spells at night. Ridiculing his accusers, Apuleius declared that being tall and handsome was hardly a crime; and as for erotic poetry, the emperor Hadrian, famously in love with the young slave boy Antinous, had written the same kind of poems, and so had the great philosopher Plato; so he was happy to stand with them, guilty as charged. Furthermore, he declared, being a philosopher, he found poverty no shame and was, in fact, indifferent to wealth; besides, he said, charges of making aphrodisiacs and practicing magic to get rich were easy ones to throw at any successful and charismatic man.[57]

Apuleius freely admitted, however, that he had learned magic and practiced magical arts; after all, he declared, Persian magic "is nothing but worship of the gods."[58] The secret rituals he practiced were, he insisted, compatible with his philosophical vocation, since they involved priestly secrets and divine wisdom. And while he laughed at the charge that he had bought fish parts to make aphrodisiacs, he allowed the courtroom audience to infer that his magic was not only sophisticated but effective, while aiming derision—and a veiled threat—against his accusers: "I am surprised that they are not afraid to attack a person they admit is so powerful."[59] As for his marriage, Apuleius first said that his accusers had exaggerated his wife's age—she was not a day over fifty-five—then he suggested that she was closer to forty (although he left this vague) and declared that "I married for love, not money."[60] Later, however, suggesting that she was sick as well as old, he hinted that it hadn't taken magic to induce the woman to marry a handsome young man; he was, indeed, quite a catch, and she was lucky to have found him.

Acquitted for lack of evidence, Apuleius wrote a famous satirical novel that gives a comic version of his "quest for secret wisdom," culminating in an account of his initiation into the cult of the goddess Isis. Earlier in the story, however, Apuleius savagely ridicules two foreign cults—that of the Syrian goddess Magna Mater ("Great Mother") and that of the Christians. Often called *The Golden Ass*,[61] his novel begins as his fictional protagonist, Lucius, sets out to learn magic and falls in love with a barmaid who allows him to spy on her mistress by looking through a bedroom keyhole as she strips naked to perform magic spells. But Lucius says that, as he watched, he turned into an ass—not metaphorically, but into an actual donkey with shaggy ears, a tail, and, as he liked to mention, a huge penis. Lucius then tells how he cavorted as a beast through dangerous and comic adventures, even having been bought, beaten, and abused by frenzied devotees of Magna Mater. Speaking as the ass forced to carry her image on his back in a ritual procession, Lucius caricatures her worshippers as madmen who castrate themselves, dress in wild colors, paint their faces, and, like whirling dervishes, dance in her honor while stabbing their arms with daggers to make the blood flow as they whip themselves into a frenzy.

Breaking loose and fleeing from these maniacs, the ass was then sold to a baker, whose wife had been seduced by another bizarre foreign cult—apparently the cult of Jesus. Lucius tells how this woman, her heart filled with evil "like some filthy latrine," despised

all the gods whom others honor, claiming that instead of our
sound religion, she had a unique god of her own, inventing
futile rituals and ceremonies, deceiving her husband, drinking wine early in the morning, and giving up her body to
continual promiscuity.[62]

Thus Apuleius caricatures a convert who refuses to worship the
gods and alienates her husband by drinking wine and participat-
ing in what Christians called "love feasts."

Although he refrains from mentioning the most outrageous
charges against Christians—that they forced initiates to plunge a
knife into a newborn baby and kill it before eating its dismem-
bered body—Apuleius' description of this ignorant and dissolute
woman suggests that Christians, like devotees of the Syrian goddess, violated Roman decency. Since Apuleius, like Justin, regards
philosophy less as an intellectual discipline than a spiritual quest,
what he finds most obnoxious is that Christians spurn what he
calls "our sound religion." What Apuleius apparently suspected—
accurately, as it turned out—was that such wholesale rejection of
the gods who supported the empire could undermine the basic
values of Roman society.

Yet as the novel concludes, it assumes a different tone, even
though the protagonist still speaks in the voice of an ass. For shortly
after Lucius tells how he escaped from the mad devotees of the Syrian goddess and of Jesus, his comic tale opens onto a powerful and
moving scene. Awakened one night by a full moon, Lucius grieves
over his wasted life, washes to purify himself, and prays to Isis,
"queen of heaven," pleading to be restored to human form. At this
point, Apuleius' story tells of spiritual transformation, as signaled

by his original title, *The Metamorphoses*. Now he brilliantly uses the animal metaphor as Lucius tells how, having been an ass, a mere animal, he comes to be transformed into a genuine human being when he receives divine revelation. For Isis graciously answers his prayer, telling him to join the sacred procession that her worshippers celebrate on her great festival day. When he does, Lucius is overjoyed to feel his shaggy coat begin to fall away and his tail vanish as her power restores him to his true human stature. Trembling with gratitude and hope, he goes to her temple to ask her priests how to prepare to receive initiation into her sacred mysteries. In an account that resonates with ardent longing, Apuleius has Lucius tell how he paid the initiation fees, took the required cold plunges into the river, and bought the necessary clothes to prepare for the ritual. When initiation day arrived, he says, he finally "approached the gates of death" and underwent a kind of ritual death, until divine power came upon him, so that he was spiritually "born again" to eternal life, and received "salvation through divine grace." [63]

Thus Apuleius' story answers the question with which his quest, like those of many seekers, had begun: what kinds of revelation are false, and which are genuine? His account suggests that the truest wisdom is offered by the priests of Isis, who plumb the depths of ancient Egyptian lore. Some literary critics, noting that Apuleius maintains an ironic tone throughout the whole narrative, have suggested that Apuleius wrote simply to entertain people by ridiculing all spiritual seekers. It's true that Apuleius maintains a certain skepticism about religious professionals throughout his story: he tells, for example, how after his first initiation, the same priests pumped him for more money in following years, offering the lure of more advanced initiations. The tone of his writing is more complex, however, than simple satire. Instead, like a sophisticated Catholic who criticizes certain practices of the Vatican, Apuleius seems to speak as a genuine devotee of Isis. Without repudiating any of his other initiations or religious affiliations, his account suggests that through her divine radiance, as through a prism, he came to see refracted all the divine light in the universe.

Revelation, then, was prized by philosophers and seekers of all kinds, whether Jews, Christians, or educated "pagans" like Apuleius, who despised both Christians and Jews. And Christians could speak of Jesus—and baptism "into Christ"—much as Apuleius spoke of initiation into Isis. About twenty years before Apuleius wrote his *Metamorphoses*, his older contemporary Justin had explained that Christian baptism offers "illumination" to the initiate who offers the requisite prayers, takes a purifying bath, and so is "born again," like those initiated into the mysteries of Isis or Mithra.[64] Furthermore, Justin praised Jesus much as Apuleius praised Isis—as the divine Word (*logos*) who sends divine illumination to everyone on earth who has ever received it, from Moses to Plato. Anyone listening to a philosopher like Justin or Apuleius might well ask, what difference could it possibly make whether one follows Plato or Jesus, worships Isis or Christ?

Christian admirers of the Book of Revelation could answer that question, since many stood in diametric opposition to the Roman world. A pagan critic like Apuleius, for all his curiosity about foreign religions, despised what he saw of theirs. Apuleius' caricature of Christians as the illiterate, low-class baker's wife shows his contempt for the majority of Christians, who lacked—or rejected—Roman culture. Ambitious and gifted men coming from the provinces, like Apuleius himself, instinctively recognized that the empire's cosmopolitanism demanded conformity to its shared values. So although he could embrace almost any kind of religious devotion, he despised foreign cults whose practices violated Roman sensibilities—the castrated priests of the Syrian goddess, and the crowd of rabble who "worship Jesus as a god."[65] Apuleius, like Celsus, despised Christians for pitching their message to the dregs of the empire. While his own initiations into the mysteries of Isis and those of Serapis, Asclepius, and Mithra required him to pay expensive initiation fees and buy special clothes for the required rituals and celebrations, practices that screened out undesirables, Christians offered baptism without payment, welcoming even beggars and slaves.[66]

In practical terms, then, Christian baptism had an effect opposite that of Isis initiation. When Apuleius devoted himself to Isis and saw all divinity encompassed by her, he embraced a universal vision, one that allowed—even encouraged—him to continue to respect and pay homage to the entire pagan pantheon, from the patron deities of Rome to the gods of Egypt, Greece, and Persia. But accepting Christian baptism, along with indoctrination into Jewish traditions about God, cut off the initiate from such universal worship. On the contrary, Christian initiation alienated everyone who received it from Rome and her gods and placed the person into a new—potentially dangerous—situation. As Apuleius noted, the Christian convert refused to worship any but her "one unique god," not only turning her back upon all other deities but damning them all as demons. Although educated Christians like Justin often prided themselves on their universalism, those on both sides realized that the difference between worshipping Isis and worshipping Jesus could make the difference between life and death.

When Tertullian confronted charges like these—that Christians played to the masses—he gleefully confirmed them. Deliberately outraging the sensibilities of his literate audience, he addressed his own subversive messages directly—even preferentially—to "the rabble." Tertullian declares that he intends to speak above all to the person who is "simple, rude, uncultured, uneducated," whose soul "belongs entirely to the road, to the street, to the workshop." Everyone instinctively seeks God, he says, but finds divine revelation not, as Plato says, through the intellect but through intuition, which is available to everyone. When it comes to knowing God, Tertullian tells his audience, being illiterate may be an advantage:

> I want your inexperience, since no one feels any confidence in you. . . . I want only what you come with, which you know from yourself, or from the author of yourself, whoever that may be.[67]

Expecting his hearer to agree that educated people are often fools, Tertullian encourages him to "have faith in your soul; thus you will believe in yourself."[68] Rejecting Plato's warning that God is hard to find, Tertullian insists that, on the contrary, "every Christian workingman finds God, and manifests God," simply by plumbing the depths of his own soul. Tertullian adds that even though "I realize that you are not a Christian,"[69] he expects his hearer to agree that, as "everyone knows," truth comes not from sophisticated elites but from ordinary working people.

Had critics like Celsus and Apuleius read Tertullian's *Apology*, they could have predicted—and would have despised—its appeal to marginal people, especially illiterates and resident aliens working in Roman cities. When Tertullian speaks to such people, he turns on its head what Romans learned as schoolboys: that the gods bestowed power and empire upon the Roman people to reward their piety. "Unless I am mistaken," he says sarcastically, "all rule and empire are gained by war and victories." Rome's conquests are actually not the reward of piety but come "from acts of impiety," including the atrocities Roman soldiers routinely practice, besieging and capturing cities, razing buildings and setting whole neighborhoods on fire, as well as terrorizing, raping, and killing innocent people and stealing the property of the slain.[70] Like atheists today who say there is no God who sanctions traditional values, Tertullian mocks those who offer sacrifice and pray that the gods will protect them, for, he says, "as you yourselves secretly know," the gods are nothing but dead men whom later generations imagine as heroes. Consequently, Roman religion is nothing but a flimsy fabric of lies.[71]

From this Tertullian concludes that Roman law, which claims divine sanction, is merely an arbitrary invention: "Your law is not right; it is only a human construct . . . it did not come down from heaven."[72] Expecting his hearers to share his alienation from Rome, Tertullian urges them to admit that instead of loving and trusting the emperor, they fear him and resent his power. Addressing workmen who carve images of the gods, hammering out their statues for huge public monuments and stamping them on coins, Tertullian says, "While you are working on the bronze image of Juno and adorning Minerva's helmet with figures, you never think of appealing to any of these gods."[73]

Tertullian dismisses such gods as masks for Rome's military

power. He invites his hearers to identify instead with Jesus, whose crucifixion showed how brutally the Romans treated subjects who resisted their power—and whose resurrection expressed their hope of seeing Rome conquered. Citing the Book of Revelation, Tertullian suggests that what "our own John" saw in heaven has opened up a region in the imagination where even now God's messiah rules as "King of kings and Lord of lords," whence he is about to descend to destroy all earthly powers. Tertullian exalts that this vision, which turns the world as he knows it upside down, gives him and countless others courage to defy the overwhelming forces that now dominate them on earth. Declaring himself a citizen of that "heavenly country," Tertullian claims that John's vision stands as a judgment against the demonic empire now ruling the world and gives him courage to stand as a free man on earth. "Never will I call the emperor 'god.' I am willing to call him 'lord,' in the ordinary sense of the term, but *my relationship to him is one of freedom.*"[74]

Emboldened by John of Patmos' vision, Tertullian demands from Roman magistrates something unprecedented—something for which he might have been the first to conceive the idea that American revolutionaries, more than fifteen centuries later, would incorporate into their new social and political system: freedom of religion, which Tertullian, writing in Latin, calls *libertate religionis.*[75] Those of us who usually think of *human rights* and *natural rights* as concepts born from the Enlightenment, wrung from the violence of the French and American revolutions, might be surprised to see this African Christian standing up to defy Scapula, the Roman magistrate stationed in Africa, circa 205 C.E., with these words: "It is a *fundamental human right, a power bestowed*

by nature, that each person should worship according to his own con-
victions, free from compulsion."[76]

Thus followers of Jesus widened the gap that Jews had originally placed between politics and religion. What Tertullian
demanded on the basis that God had created the human soul
American revolutionaries would claim on similar grounds, alluding to the Genesis creation account to insist, in 1776, that *"all men*
are created equal, and endowed by their creator with certain inalien-
able rights."[77] Tertullian, of course, was speaking of freedom for
Christians, and hoped for it only after Rome's downfall, when, as
John had prophesied, Christ would descend in glory to reign over
the new Jerusalem. But what actually happened was something
that the fierce prophet John, for all his visions of the future, could
hardly have foreseen.

CHAPTER FIVE

Constantine's Conversion:
How John's Revelation Became Part of the Bible

The fourth century began in a decade of terror. Rome was now "making war" on Jesus' followers, just as John of Patmos had prophesied that "the beast" would do. On February 23, 303, the emperor Diocletian ordered his soldiers to destroy churches, confiscate and burn their sacred books, and strip anyone who resisted of civil rights, status, and police protection. This edict was enforced throughout much of the empire but most seriously in Egypt, where Christians experienced increasingly systematic persecution.[1] A few months later, Diocletian sent another edict ordering magistrates to arrest church leaders and use any means necessary to force them to sacrifice to the gods. Christian leaders were divided on how to respond. Peter, bishop of Alexandria, went into hiding and commended others who fled or bribed officials to avoid apostasy, saying that this showed that they loved God more than their money. While many Christians found such ways to accommodate the laws and survive, others, like Bishop Melitius of Lycopolis, a city in Upper Egypt, urged believers to resist Rome and accept death rather than either comply with the laws or evade them. During the seven years between 303 and 310, Christians in Alexandria reported that 660 of their own were killed in that city alone.[2]

Many Christians who suffered torture or saw fellow believers blinded in their right eye—the sockets seared with hot irons—

and the tendons of their left ankles burned, scorched, and disabled, could see in those grim days signs of the end that John of Patmos had prophesied. But no one, certainly not John, had he been alive, could have expected what happened next. What came to an end was not *the world*, but *persecution*—in astonishing ways. The first hint of a reprieve came in the spring of 311, when Christians heard that the dreaded emperors had issued an edict of toleration offering imperial clemency "so that Christians may again exist," on the condition that "they do nothing contrary to good order."[3] When Bishop Peter heard that the danger had passed, he gladly ended seven years in exile and returned to Alexandria. About six months later, however, the emperor Maximinus, who ruled the East, countermanded the previous edict and sent secret orders to imperial soldiers, who suddenly arrested Peter and hastily tried, tortured, and killed him.[4] Then, by a miracle, many said, less than a year later, on October 28, 312, Constantine, son of one of the imperial rulers, anticipating battle the next morning against his rivals for imperial power, suddenly adopted Christ as his patron. As Eusebius, bishop of Caesarea, in Palestine, heard the story, Constantine said later that he had seen a great omen in the sky, and then in a dream, that promised him victory through Christ's sign.[5] Constantine ordered a copy of that sign—a staff with letters indicating Christ's name— to be emblazoned on a banner and carried before his army, and under this sign he defeated and killed Maxentius, his rival emperor in the West. The next day he entered Rome in triumph, hailed as emperor. Shortly afterward, Constantine and his co-regent, Licinius, published an edict declaring Christianity a legal religion and allowing what Tertullian had only dared imagine—each person free to worship "as seems good to him."[6]

During the following decades, Constantine sought to shift the empire toward Christianity, as he saw it. Among many other edicts, he exempted Christian clergy from taxation and granted them power to enact legal transactions. He outlawed crucifixion as a legal punishment, repealed legal disabilities for the unmarried, introduced stricter divorce legislation, and prohibited gladiatorial shows as public entertainment.[7]

Now that Constantine's Rome was becoming, in effect, a *Christian* empire, we might expect that the Book of Revelation would fade into obscurity, its prophecies having been proved wrong—but this did not happen either. Although many Christians preferred to leave the book behind, others chose to not give up these vivid and compelling visions. Instead they reinterpreted them, as Christians have done ever since. After Constantine's victory, those who seized upon John's prophecies for their own times often insisted that people who read them literally—or differently—failed to understand them. The Egyptian bishop Athanasius was the first, so far as we know, to place the Book of Revelation in his version of the New Testament canon, when he saw how to use it as a weapon—not against Rome and its rulers but against *other Christians* whom he called heretics.[8]

Now that Constantine had ended persecution, Christians began to contend among themselves more intensely than ever. The emperor's favor enormously raised the stakes, for after he took Christ as his patron, Constantine opened his imperial treasuries to rebuild churches previously targeted for destruction. Christian clergy, once hunted and haunted by fear and memories of those horribly killed, now received tax exemptions and special privileges. Those who had been tortured or enslaved, or whose homes and property had been confiscated, received promises of full restitution. Now Constantine openly preferred Christians when making official appointments and began to treat bishops virtually as his agents, placing tax money at their disposal, giving them the right to free slaves and judge legal cases, and even handing over to the bishop of Alexandria control of much of the city's grain supply. So while Peter, who previously held that position, had been targeted and killed because of his prominence, his successors fought to gain the position, which could make its possessor a rich and powerful man.[9]

Christians newly thrust into leadership competed for the emperor's favor, now a prerequisite for securing a major position. After the year 312, when Constantine first declared his preference for Christianity, he had chosen to become the patron of those Christians who called themselves *catholic* (from the Greek for "universal"). Within a few years he had adopted their practice of calling all other Christian groups, along with their clergy, *heretics*—that is, in effect, sectarians—who, he now declared, had no legal right to meet for worship, even in private homes, much less to own churches. In 324 he "legislated an end to all heretical sects"[10] and ordered that their property be confiscated and turned over to Catholic Christians. His successors would impose strict sanctions on Jews as well.

Constantine, concerned with managing his enormous empire, noted with approval that Catholic clergy had adopted the Roman army's system of rank, command, and promotion to create effective control over a wide network of congregations. In this way, Christian leaders Romanized Christianity, while Christianizing Rome. In Egypt, for example, the Catholic bishop of Alexandria claimed responsibility for all Christians in the capital city and over all bishops identified as *catholic* throughout Egypt, designating each, like himself, to supervise a specific area called a *diocese* and to take charge of two lower ranks, called *priests* and *deacons* (from the Greek terms for "elders" and "servants"), while maintaining communication with the whole network.

Yet in spite of Constantine's patronage, such bishops often encountered fierce resistance when they tried to control other bishops and their congregations—for example, those who remained loyal to Bishop Melitius of Lycopolis, who had quarreled with Bishop Peter, and also to control monks and other believers loyal to a host of independent leaders and groups. Sometimes bishops loyal to Constantine encountered challenges even from their own congregations and clergy. About ten years after Constantine sought to support a unified church, he was frustrated to hear that violence had broken out between Christians in Egypt. Some say the trouble began when Alexander, the Catholic bishop of Alexandria, publicly challenged what Arius, a popular Libyan priest in his diocese, preached about Jesus, setting off angry controversy.[11] Constantine wrote to both Bishop Alexander and the priest Arius, urging them to recognize that Christians could disagree about details of doctrine while maintaining brotherly love within the same "universal" church, and warning that public arguments only caused harm and showed ingratitude for the freedom and privileges they now enjoyed.[12] Constantine wrote that he had investigated the cause of their dispute and found it "extremely trivial, and quite unworthy of so much controversy," especially since it set "so many of God's people" in conflict "because you are quarreling with each other about small and quite minute points."[13]

The initial dispute involved different views of Jesus' divinity: whether what in him was divine was "essentially the same as God." The New Testament accounts do not answer such questions, which their authors apparently did not ask in the ways that fourth-century theologians did. The gospels of Mark, Matthew, and Luke tend to support the view of Jesus as a human being divinely chosen as God's messiah, although they contain hints later used by some Christians to support the claim that the divine Word incarnate in Jesus was "essentially the same as God." Those who insisted on the latter view supported their position by drawing primarily upon Paul's letters and the Gospel of John, although people on both sides used passages from John's gospel to argue their views.[14] When both sides sought support from bishops throughout the eastern provinces, threatening schism, Constantine called a conference to settle the dispute. Since he ruled primarily in the East, not in Rome, he convened more than two hundred bishops—one bishop claimed there had been more than three hundred[15]—from Egypt, Palestine, Syria, and as far away as Rome to meet in Nicea, in Asia Minor, in June 325. The Egyptian bishop Alexander of Alexandria helped set the agenda, working with other bishops and with his eighteen-year-old secretary, Athanasius, to draft a complex set of dogmatic propositions that Athanasius insisted was "the truth necessary for salvation."[16] The final version of the creedal statement they drafted, called the Nicene Creed, upheld, above all, the disputed view that although Jesus was human, what in him was divine was "of one being with the Father," or, if we translate the crucial term *homoousios* differently, "essentially the same as" God.[17]

Constantine greeted the bishops at Nicea in person, addressed the meeting, and sat among them during the deliberations. After hearing hours of debate, which he seemed to feel was squabbling over details, he strongly endorsed the document's wording and urged its acceptance. At that point, nearly all the assembled church leaders agreed to sign the document, except for Arius himself and two Libyan bishops associated with him, who, having been cut off from communion with the Catholic Church and ordered into exile, hastily departed. Because the pragmatic Constantine chose to defer to the bishops as experts in matters of faith, he and some of his successors came to treat the theological formulations of this document as a litmus test of orthodoxy. Christians who agreed to accept the Nicene Creed were entitled to share in the special exemptions and legal privileges awarded to Catholic Christians, while those who questioned or rejected it outright could be cut off and excluded—not only from earthly advantages but also from eternal ones, since many agreed with what Bishop Irenaeus had declared two centuries earlier: that "outside the church there is no salvation."

Although the assembled bishops continued to meet at Nicea for more than another month in order to take up other disputed issues, their meeting failed to resolve the divisions between churches that had begun during the persecutions. For as we noted, after Bishop Peter of Alexandria had fled the capital city and urged other believers to save their lives, he clashed with Bishop Melitius, who, having boldly "confessed" to being Christian, was sentenced and sent to hard labor in the mines. In 311, when persecution ended, Melitius returned to Alexandria with the prestige of having risked martyrdom,[18] a stand that had gained him a loyal following of twenty-eight bishops, along with their clergy and congregations, in thirty cities and towns along the Nile. The majority of bishops at Nicea, however, sought to reintegrate his followers into the Catholic Church of Egypt by voting for compromise. They agreed to confirm Melitius' status as bishop of Lycopolis and to accept priests he already had ordained as validly consecrated, but they also voted to forbid him to ordain any more. Finally, they ruled that clergy loyal to Melitius henceforth should be subordinated to Bishop Peter's successor, Alexander.

Having gained this support from the emperor and the council, Alexander effectively won the right to supervise not only the churches in Alexandria but those in all of Egypt. Three years later, Alexander died unexpectedly, and while a council of more than fifty bishops gathered to choose his successor, seven others met separately and ordained Athanasius, the former bishop's young secretary, as the new head bishop. This outcome was intensely disputed.[19] Those opposed to Athanasius objected that he was not even a priest and, at age twenty-eight, below the minimum age requirement for a bishop; furthermore, some charged that he had engineered his own ordination.[20] Athanasius quickly sent a message to Constantine announcing that the people of Alexandria had chosen him as bishop, quoting a decree from the city council as proof. His supporters later defended their choice by insisting that not only had Bishop Alexander himself, before he died, designated Athanasius to succeed him, but the people of Alexandria had enthusiastically endorsed Athanasius as their candidate.

Bishops loyal to Melitius immediately challenged Athanasius by electing a bishop of their own. To their shock, however, the emperor effectively ratified Athanasius' election when he sent a message congratulating him. With this victory, Athanasius confronted the challenge that would engage him for the next forty-six years: how to weld the disparate believers and groups throughout Egypt into a single, Catholic (that is, "universal") communion. It was easier for the emperor to write imperial orders than for others to enforce them—a task left primarily to the bishops, since the emperor ruled from afar, occupied with many other pressing matters. Yet, as we shall see, besides schismatic priests and bishops, Athanasius also confronted thousands of Christians in Egypt, many in the monastic movement, who had remained independent of his ecclesiastical hierarchy and, in some cases, of *any* clergy. How, then, could Athanasius induce all Christians in Egypt to conform to the complex formulas expressed in the Nicene Creed and herd these various believers all over Egypt into a single "flock" headed by himself, as bishop of Alexandria?[21]

During his long struggle to accomplish this, Athanasius found an unlikely ally in John of Patmos—especially as Irenaeus had read him. For as we noted, Irenaeus interpreted God's enemies, whom John had pictured as the "beast" and the "whore," to refer not only to Rome's rulers but also to *Christians* deceived, by the false teacher he called Antichrist, into false doctrine and into committing evil. Apparently familiar with earlier Jewish traditions about such an "antimessiah" (which translates as "antichrist" from Greek), Irenaeus linked these falsifiers with John's visions of the beast, to warn of the danger to God's people from within the churches as well as from the outside.[22] Athanasius, who had found an ally in the emperor Constantine, initially omitted any reference to "the beast" as embodied in Roman rulers. Instead he emphasized Irenaeus' view that those who follow "the beast" (whom he, too, identified with Antichrist) are actually those Christians whom he called heretics.

During his forty-six years as bishop, Athanasius was deposed and sent into exile *five times*. Since doctrinal tradition was not yet fixed, bishops who supported Arius and regarded Athanasius as the heretic voted to depose him, and sometimes succeeded in persuading Constantine and his sons to replace him with bishops from their own ranks. But each time, Athanasius sought and found supporters throughout the empire and wrote furiously, often from exile, against his opponents. His admirers saw him as a man courageous enough to take on the whole world—"Athanasius against the world," they called him—while his opponents characterized him as "a rich and powerful man, capable of anything."[23] Athanasius campaigned tirelessly against Christians who questioned or qualified the phrases in the Nicene Creed, calling them Arians, to imply that they were not real Christians but only schismatic followers of the exiled priest Arius. In return, at various times throughout his career, his enemies accused Athanasius of everything from preventing shipments of grain to be sent from Alexandria to Constantinople to violently attacking his opponents—even of having arranged the murder of a hostile bishop named Arsenius. While both sides sometimes resorted to violence,[24] Athanasius insisted that these charges were absurd. When Arsenius turned up alive, Athanasius declared himself vindicated and called on his supporters

> to fight for the truth unto death; to abominate the Arian heresy, which fights against Christ, and is a forerunner of Antichrist, and not to believe those who try to speak against me.[25]

When Constantine died and his son Constantius took power, Athanasius' opponents redoubled their efforts to unseat the powerful bishop. The young emperor attended a council of bishops held in Antioch in 338, which confirmed the decision of a council held the previous year, in which the bishops sided with Arius and his supporters and voted to depose Athanasius. Constantius ordered Athanasius to vacate his office and go into exile. Defiant, Athanasius remained in Alexandria until the magistrates sought to arrest him; then he fled the city and left Egypt. Later, writing from exile, Athanasius declared that his opponents, of whatever party, were not Christians at all but "the devil's people,"[26] whom he derisively called by the names of their leaders. Those loyal to Melitius, he said, were just as bad as Arius' supporters, because "Melitians and Arians mingle their respective errors like the cup of Babylon."[27] Thus, as the conflict intensified, Athanasius increasingly interpreted the *whore* of Babylon, who drinks human blood, no longer as *Rome* but rather as *heresy personified*. Writing his own version of conflict over the Nicene Creed, Athanasius charged that those he called heretics "want to . . . shed my blood!"[28]

During these protracted battles, Athanasius challenged Bishop Melitius, who had criticized Athanasius' predecessor, Bishop Peter, for hiding during the persecutions. Since Melitius had supervised the churches during Peter's absence, he claimed to represent "the church of the martyrs," implying that Peter had disqualified himself as bishop by fleeing the city. Now, some thirty years later, Athanasius had to compete with Melitius' followers for the favor of the new emperor, Constantine's son Constantius. Athanasius charged that his opponents were opportunists who would do anything to gain a bishop's new prerogatives—tax exemptions and imperial patronage. When Constantius supported Arius' teaching and promoted Melitius' followers, Athanasius wrote mockingly that "from being Melitians, they eagerly and quickly became Arians."[29] Still writing from exile, Athanasius insisted that the bishops who replaced him and his allies had been chosen "because of the wealth and civil power they possessed," as well as the bribes that he said they offered, so that "when Antichrist comes, he shall find that the churches in Egypt are already his own."[30]

During this controversy, Athanasius raised a basic question: *how could an emperor validate a bishop?*[31] Ignoring his own early appeal for Constantine's support for his election, he asked rhetorically: when did Christian churches ever recognize a magistrate's order? Above all, how could they obey *Constantius'* orders, after he had "commanded Athanasius to be expelled from the city and publicly ordered that the bishops of the Catholic faith be thrown out of their churches, and that they all be given up to those professing Arian teachings"? Athanasius dared accuse the emperor Constantius not only of clearing the way for Antichrist but of having *become* Antichrist himself: "How can he fail to be regarded as Antichrist?"[32]

Like Bishop Irenaeus two centuries earlier,[33] Athanasius turned John's visions of cosmic war into a weapon against those he called heretics—"Melitians," "Arians," or, in his favorite phrase, "Ariomaniacs," who "fight against Christ." Athanasius insisted that Constantine had been right to promote the council at Nicea as uniquely valid, since there, he said, "all the fathers" had supported the true faith against the "Antichristian heresy." When living in an empire ruled by a Christian who supported his Arian opponents, then, Athanasius interpreted John's Book of Revelation as condemning all "heretics," and then made this book the capstone of the New Testament canon, where it has remained ever since. At the same time, he ordered Christians to stop reading any *other* "books of revelation," which he branded heretical and sought to destroy—with almost complete success.

For although Irenaeus, in his massive book *Against Heresies*, had denounced such "secret books" two hundred years earlier, Athanasius knew that many Christians in Egypt either were unaware of that ancient warning or ignored it.[34] Many continued to copy and read such books for devotional use, even translating them into Coptic to make them more accessible. Athanasius had heard, too, that in some monasteries monks read and discussed such "secret books" both in private and in their communal devotions. These books have remained largely unknown, since nearly all copies were destroyed as heretical after the fourth century; but the cache of more than fifty so-called Gnostic gospels and "secret books" found in 1945 at Nag Hammadi, in Upper Egypt, survived Athanasius' order. Although we don't know exactly who hid them there or where they had previously been kept,[35] they had been buried in a sealed jar within walking distance of three monasteries, near caves where monks went to meditate and pray.

Athanasius realized that in order to unite all Christians in Egypt under his leadership, he would have to take on the monasteries, and this would not be easy. Many of these monasteries had sprung up throughout Egypt independent of any centralized church authority; some monks, too, looked to monastery leaders and spiritual teachers, not bishops, for direction.[36] Athanasius knew that many other Christians also sought God in ways not directly connected with Catholic Christianity and that they treasured "secret books" loosely associated with teachings of the Egyptian Christian teacher Origen, with philosophers like Plato and Plotinus, and even with traditions associated with the Egyptian goddess Isis and the Greek god Hermes. Athanasius' project committed him and his clergy to power struggles that would engage him for the rest of his life.

The monastic movement had flourished throughout Egypt, especially in rural areas, ever since Constantine first legalized Christianity. Even before Constantine, Christians told stories of great spiritual heroes and sought to emulate them—men and women who left ordinary life behind, choosing to seclude themselves at home or in shelters clustered outside of towns or to go into the barren desert to search for God. Such stories told how these ascetics took on rigorous physical and spiritual disciplines as "exercise" (*ascesis*, in Greek), since they saw themselves as "athletes for God." Although such seekers often sought advice from older ascetics, and many gathered on Sundays to worship with others living nearby, they called themselves "solitaries," or "single ones" (in Greek, *monachoi*, later translated as "monks"),[37] since they had given up family life to practice celibacy.

Stories of Anthony of Egypt, one of the pioneers of the movement, told how, as a young man, he had "left the world" of his village to live in solitude for decades, first in a cemetery, then in a desert shelter, until his visions and reputation for holiness had spawned legends, and countless Christians sought him out as their mentor. Some hunters, too, told how, having met one of those solitary seekers in the desert and asked what he was doing there, he replied, "I'm a hunter too—I'm hunting for my God." Others told of the "old man" Lot, who, when questioned, stood up and raised his fingers "like ten torches of fire" and said, "If you are willing, you can become a living flame!"[38]

When Athanasius was still a boy, shortly after Constantine legalized Christianity, an ex-soldier named Pachomius, inspired by such stories, set out to devote his life to God. Pachomius had been conscripted into the Roman army during the 290s and had first met Christians when some of them brought food and comfort to the new soldiers, then billeted in a cold and drafty camp in Upper Egypt. After Pachomius' release from the army in 313, he sought baptism. Yet much as he admired stories of courageous hermits, Pachomius hesitated to follow their example. Hadn't Jesus urged his followers to "love one another"? And couldn't one build an actual society on that principle? Pachomius said he had received a divine revelation telling him to build a communal house that he hoped would become an outpost of heaven on earth. Claiming his vision's guidance, he urged others seeking God not to live simply as "solitaries" but as members of a spiritual community. Pachomius persuaded a few followers to work with him and build a mud-and-brick house that could accommodate several hundred men, a building later called by the paradoxical term *monasterium*—in effect, a "community of solitaries."[39]

After they finished building, Pachomius, acting as "father" (*abba*), set up for the "brothers" who joined him a rotating schedule of work, prayer, and worship, while he himself cooked and served their meals and supervised the whole group. Several years later, after this communal house had attracted many more rural Egyptians, including many experiencing economic hardship, by offering shelter, food, and work in the setting of a spiritual family, Pachomius traveled to a village near Nag Hammadi to supervise the building of a much larger monastery. This one, built to house thousands of volunteers, would later become the headquarters of a network of nine monasteries that he and his staff would supervise along the Upper Nile, along with two affiliated communities of women. For women, too, had joined the movement, some living together in large private houses, others in monasteries built for them. Each group worked to sustain itself economically while remaining in contact with the whole federation, which Pachomius named "the Community" (*koinonia*, in Greek).

At the large communal house near Nag Hammadi, fifty miles north of present-day Luxor, some monks worked in the fields to raise lentils, okra, and grain, while others washed clothes, cleaned rooms, cooked, baked bread, and wove baskets and rope to sell at markets in town to support the community's needs. New recruits who arrived knowing how to read and write worked in a room set aside as a library. Some copied Coptic manuscripts of the Scriptures and other writings, while those who knew Greek translated sacred writings from Greek into Coptic to be read to the whole community. Later tradition reports that such recruits were expected to teach illiterate brothers to work through some of the Psalms and the New Testament, or at least memorize large passages from both, so that they could better participate in worship and devotions. We do not know whether what we call the Nag Hammadi texts came from this monastery, as seems likely;[40] but we can reconstruct how such books were read. For after finishing the day's work and the evening meal of bread, vegetables, olives, and water, the community would gather for devotions, as Pachomius or another experienced monk would open in prayer, then speak to them and read aloud from sacred books.

As evening darkened into night, a newcomer seated among his monastic "brothers" might hear sacred readings from the Scriptures and, since no New Testament canon had yet been codified, also from books that Athanasius would condemn as "heretical."[41] As the reader opened the heavy leather cover of Codex I, one of the thirteen volumes found at Nag Hammadi, and began to read the Prayer of the Apostle Paul, written on the flyleaf, a newcomer listening to evening devotions might have shared in the intense expectation it expresses:

> My Redeemer, redeem me, for I am yours, having come forth from you; you are my mind, bring me forth! You are my treasury; open for me! You are my fullness; take me to you! . . . Grant what "no angel's eye has seen; what no . . . ear has heard; what has not entered into the human heart."[42]

This prayer speaks to those who long for communion with God, and who hope to glimpse what the apostle Paul called "the deep things of God."[43] The reader would probably conclude with the exclamation that the scribe had added to the prayer—"Christ is holy!" Then, turning to the Secret Revelation of James on the next page, he might begin to speak, in effect, in the words of Jesus' brother James as he answers a seeker's request

> that I send you a secret book [apocryphon] that was revealed to me and Peter by the Lord, and I could neither deter nor

deny you what you ask; but I have written it in Hebrew, and have sent it to you, and you alone.[44]

Excited by these words, a novice would have listened more intently for the secrets James is about to reveal. As he listened, he might have heard "the living Jesus" invite him to join Peter, James, and John to *seek revelation*: "I am the one who is with you always" . . . "If you want to come with me, come!"[45]

Having joined the inner circle of believers in the monastery, the novice then might hear such readings, which invite—and challenge—believers to go beyond the elementary teaching that they might have heard at churches in town. For listening to this "secret revelation" and others,[46] one might hear oneself included among disciples allowed to hear what these writings claim Jesus spoke in private: "From now on . . . remember that you have seen the Son of Man, and spoken with him in person, and listened to him in person. . . . Become better than I; make yourselves like the son of the Holy Spirit!"[47]

Instead of being told that one can learn about Jesus only from what the apostles wrote and handed down in their writings, the Secret Revelation of James invites the believer to commune directly with "the living Jesus"—even challenges one to become *like* him. Rather than being put off with simple answers, the novice is encouraged to ask bolder questions: What was there before the world was created? Where do we come from, and where are we going? How can we come to know God—not just through Bible stories or concepts but *experientially*—and come to know who, spiritually speaking, we really are?

The newcomer might have to wait for the next session, on

another night, to hear readings from the Gospel of Truth, which follows next in the same volume and speaks to these questions, offering to reveal "the true gospel." The Gospel of Truth begins by telling how, "in the beginning," all beings came forth from the Father, but then lost contact with their divine source and so fell into anguish and terror, like people lost in dense fog. But this gospel, weaving in allusions to the New Testament Gospel of John, goes on to tell how the Father sent his Son into the world to bring his lost and lonely children back into the embrace of divine love, "into the Father, into the Mother, Jesus of the infinite sweetness."[48]

Leaving aside more familiar teachings about Christ as the "lamb of God" offered as atonement, as a sacrifice to "save us from our sins,"[49] the Gospel of Truth, like the New Testament Gospel of John, pictures Jesus' crucifixion as *itself* a revelation—one that reveals God's love and shows us who we really are.[50] Recalling the tree of knowledge in Paradise, this gospel pictures Jesus "nailed to a tree," as the "fruit" that offers *true* knowledge, "the fruit of knowing the Father." Those who "eat this fruit" by sharing in worship the bread and wine that recall Jesus' death discover that they share an intimate connection with God, and become "glad in the discovery; for he discovered them in himself, and they discovered him in themselves."[51] As the reader concludes, those listening in the dark might feel themselves blessed, now that they have been called back into communion with God as "the children ... that he loves."[52]

Yet those reflecting on the poetic images of Jesus' crucifixion in the Gospel of Truth might also wonder about the question that opens the next writing—a question many Christians ask to this day: *Is it necessary to believe that Jesus was actually raised from the dead?* The anonymous author of the Letter to Rheginos (also called Treatise on the Resurrection) writes to a student who has asked this question, saying that although it is difficult to answer, "let us discuss the matter."[53] Anyone struggling with this question would know, of course, that certain disciples had said they *had* seen Jesus alive after his death and that certain gospel stories suggest that he had come back *physically*.[54] Some stories report that his disciples had actually touched and felt his body—even, as the Book of Acts says Peter claimed, that he and others "ate and drank with him after he rose from the dead."[55]

Rheginos' teacher answers *yes* in his letter: one must believe in resurrection—but not *literally*. Recalling what Paul teaches about resurrection, he explains that it does not necessarily mean resuscitation of the present physical body, since "flesh and blood cannot inherit the kingdom of God, nor can corruption inherit incorruption."[56] Although, as he points out, the apostle Paul says that resurrection is a mystery, Rheginos' teacher insists that faith in it is neither optional nor an illusion; on the contrary, "it is the truth"— more real than the world in which we now live! He goes on to say that although it is not easy to understand, *resurrection* shows how we, once oblivious to divine reality, may be raised to spiritual life and become enlightened: "Why not think of yourself as raised, then, and already brought to this?"[57] Resurrection, then, involves a shift in consciousness—it is "the revelation of what is, and the transformation of things, and a transition into newness."[58] But, Rheginos' teacher cautions, "if someone doesn't believe it, my son, the person cannot be persuaded," since resurrection is a matter of faith, not philosophical argument.

Hearing such sources read aloud, most likely on successive nights—in gatherings for devotions that might conclude with the group praying together and sometimes embracing before sharing the sacred meal[59]—the novice might be moved to hear the final teaching in Codex I speak poetically of whence we came and where we are going. For the Tripartite Tractate that concludes the book we call Codex I expands what the Gospel of Truth had sketched out: how, in the beginning, each of us—and all beings in the universe—came forth from God, the Father, "like a young child, like a drop of water from a spring, like a blossom from a vine."[60] Although originally all were linked together, the Tripartite Tractate, like the Gospel of Truth, tells how they became scattered and separated, then turned arrogant and violent, lusting for power, fighting to dominate and kill one another, as people do in the outside world. Those gathered in the monastery, hearing this account, could see themselves as God's children, whom Christ had brought back and joined into one community so that, as this final teaching concludes, they might "help one another" as they seek to be reunited with "the One filled with love, through his holy spirit, from now through all generations, forever and ever. Amen."[61]

On other nights, in spring or winter, the monks might listen to teachings from other sacred books from the monastery library. As we have seen, such writings as the Secret Revelation of James offer techniques of prayer drawn from Jewish tradition to lift heart, mind, and spirit, while the Discourse on the Eighth and Ninth and Allogenes set forth disciplines of fasting, study, meditation, and prayer practiced in Hermetic, Platonic, and perhaps Buddhist circles as well, to help attune body, mind, and spirit. For, as one famous disciple of Plato had said, one who seeks God waits for a voice [one] longs to hear: he ignores all other sounds, and attunes his ear to listen for that sound ... keeping the soul's conscious power pure and ready to hear the sounds from above.[62]

Just as Christian monks today often include in their libraries books written by teachers ranging from the Dalai Lama to the Jewish master Moses Maimonides, monks in such monasteries as those in Upper Egypt apparently gathered eclectic writings for their libraries.[63]

Some scholars who first read these texts after their discovery in 1945, noting how they diverge from orthodox tradition, assumed that monks would have collected such writings only to refute the heresy they found in them. More recent research suggests, however, that early in the fourth century, before Athanasius' campaign to reform the monasteries had succeeded in making them conform their teaching to orthodox doctrine, many monks might have seen these diverse writings pointing in the same direction as the great pioneers of their own monastic tradition. Athanasius knew, of course, that monks in the federation based at Nag Hammadi looked above all to Pachomius, their monastic "father," who urged them to press into the unknown, seeking the Holy Spirit's guidance, as he did himself, while countless others looked to Anthony of Egypt, that great pioneer of the spiritual life.

Anthony, born in Egypt around 250, had given up the wealth and hundreds of acres of land he had inherited when his parents died to live alone in the desert seeking God. In his later years, after he had become a mentor to monks all over Egypt and a legend throughout the empire, he wrote letters addressed to his "dear children" who sought to follow his example.[64] Anthony encouraged them to undertake "fasts, vigils, exertions and bodily disciplines" until "the guiding spirit begins to open the eyes of the soul," since the purpose of such exercises was to discover one's true self in God.[65]

What Anthony taught resonated with what Pachomius' monks might have heard in their evening devotions, as well as in the "secret writings" that Athanasius sought to dismiss. Anthony spoke of how, being created in God's image, "we are all created from one invisible being,"[66] but having lost our original connection with the divine source, we "descended into the abyss, being completely dead," and came into present existence as into a "dark house full of war."[67] Anthony went on to teach that Christ, moved by God's love, came, suffered, and died to bring us back to life. Thus, like the anonymous teacher of the Letter to Rheginos, Anthony wrote that God's spirit resurrects us—not our mortal bodies but our essential being—so that we may live in joyful communion with one another and with God. Discovering this, we may learn, with difficulty, to live by the guidance of the Holy Spirit, who restores us to ourselves—for, as Anthony wrote, "whoever knows himself, knows God."[68]

Although influenced by Plato and by the brilliant Christian teacher Origen, Anthony speaks in these letters to his "brothers and sisters" with utter simplicity, stressing the practical results of living the "angelic life": "whoever harms his neighbor harms himself . . . but whoever knows himself knows all things . . . and whoever is able to love himself loves all."[69] Because what matters most is receiving the Holy Spirit's guidance and coming to know oneself, Anthony offers no doctrines that he requires believers to learn, and no beliefs that he demands they accept. Instead, as the scholar Samuel Rubenson says, since "the chief criterion is experience," Anthony "invites and implores the reader to discover and understand himself."[70]

What listeners might hear, then, in such readings from Codex I, found at Nag Hammadi, is much the same. Like Anthony, the anonymous authors whose writings are included offer nothing to memorize, no theological systems buttressed with philosophical argument, nor any prescribed method of interpreting the Scriptures. For them, as for Anthony, "what counts is not intellectual capacity . . . but a state of mind characterized by insight and true perception."[71] Whoever collected for the monastery library such writings as the Secret Revelation of James, the Gospel of Truth, and the Letter to Rheginos, as well as the Scriptures themselves, apparently saw them not as maps but as trustworthy guides for those willing to leap into the unknown and to seek, as the spiritual teacher Origen had urged, to "be transformed!"[72]

When Athanasius set out to unify Christians all over Egypt into a single communion, then, he had to deal not only with Pachomius' federation, which had expanded by 360 c.e. to include twelve[73] communities housing thousands of men and women, but also with another network of monasteries initially loyal to his old rival Melitius, as well as lesser-known groups of Christians living in private houses, individual shelters, and monasteries that have left fewer traces.[74] Leaders in such groups, as well as freelance teachers and "fathers" like Pachomius, tended to resist attempts to intervene in their affairs, much less to control them. As monks set out to build new houses in territory that bishops and priests claimed as their own dioceses, they often clashed with the Catholic clergy. When, for example, Pachomius began to build his large monastery near Nag Hammadi, Bishop Serapion, who presided in the nearby town of Tentyra, asked Athanasius to seize Pachomius and forcibly ordain him as a priest so that he would have to subordinate himself—along with his thousands of monks—to Serapion's authority.[75] But Pachomius, determined to protect his communities' full autonomy,[76] refused ordination. Historian David Brakke notes that some time later, when Pachomius planned to build a church in Tentyra, the bishop strongly opposed this move, which could drain tribute and revenues from townspeople whom he regarded as under his own jurisdiction. And when Pachomius sought to expand to the south by starting to build a new monastery near Latopolis, the bishop of that city "led a mob in a violent attempt to stop [him]."[77]

Because Pachomius usually initiated new building projects by saying that a divine voice or an angel had told him to do so, clergy who opposed his expansionist moves accused him of receiving "revelations" from Satan, not God. In 346, a council of bishops and their allies summoned him to Latopolis to answer charges that he used "suspicious clairvoyant powers," suggesting that he was demon-possessed. Pachomius later said that he barely escaped from that trial—and from a hostile monk who chased him, wielding a sword—with his life.

When Athanasius sought to overcome resistance from monastic establishments, he chose a more effective strategy than accusing their most respected leaders of demonic possession. Instead he effectively co-opted the most famous of them—Anthony—by writing an admiring biography picturing Anthony as his own greatest supporter. Since Anthony had died, Athanasius had a

somewhat free hand, and his biography turned Anthony into a
model monk—a model, that is, of what the *bishop* wanted monks
to be. For in his famous *Life of Anthony*, the sophisticated and
fiercely independent teacher known from his letters disappears,
and Athanasius replaces him with his own vision of an ideal
monk—an illiterate and simple man.[78] So while Anthony's letters
show him to be educated in philosophy and theology, Athanasius
pictures him as someone who despises educated teachers as arrogant men who are ignorant of God. And although in his letters
Anthony never mentions bishops, clergy, or church rules, Athanasius pictures him instead as a humble monk who willingly
subordinates himself to the clergy and "the canon of the church."
Athanasius also depicts Anthony as one who hates Christian dissidents as much as he did—and who, like the bishop himself, calls
them not only *heretics* but "forerunners of Antichrist."[79] Far from
acting as an independent spiritual mentor, Athanasius' Anthony
pleads with the bishop to not allow anyone to revere him, especially after his death. As the biography ends, Athanasius pictures
Anthony bequeathing all that he has—his sheepskin cloak and
his outer garment—to Athanasius and the bishop's trusted ally,
Bishop Serapion of Thumis, to show that Anthony regarded them
as his spiritual heirs and trusted them to guard his memory.

Athanasius' *Life of Anthony* became hugely popular and widely
read throughout the empire, even inspiring Saint Augustine and
his friends, who read it in Italy long after Athanasius wrote it, to
become monks themselves; it continues to influence people who
choose monasticism even today. Athanasius did not stop with his
Life of Anthony, but went on to take more active measures to influence, and finally control, the monasteries. When Pachomius died

of plague in 346, plunging the federation into a leadership crisis, Athanasius intervened. The dying Pachomius had surprised his followers by overlooking his protégé Theodore, perhaps suspecting that he might ally with the bishops, and named instead an older monk named Petronius to succeed him. When Petronius died three months later, he, too, bypassed Theodore and designated a monk named Horsisius as the monastery's next "father." But after four difficult years, Horsisius was forced to resign. We do not know exactly why. Some said he resigned voluntarily, in tears, after a monastery administrator had refused to obey him; others noted that his rival Theodore, who would succeed him, had sought and gained the support of Athanasius before taking over as leader.[80] Unlike Pachomius, who had tended to avoid Athanasius,[81] Theodore, widely regarded as more pragmatic, had maintained frequent contact with the bishop. When Theodore finally took charge as leader of the federation, he formalized connections between the monastic federation and the church hierarchy, deferentially addressing Bishop Athanasius, along with the deceased Pachomius, as "our father"—that is, as a respected mentor from whom he accepted direction.

A few years later, in 367, when Athanasius wrote a famous Easter letter telling Christians what henceforth they could hear, teach, and discuss—and what to censor—Theodore gathered his monks together and had the bishop's letter read aloud. Recognizing that the bishop's letter mandated major change, Theodore had it written out in large letters on the monastery wall. In that letter Athanasius first denounced "spiritual teachers," especially those respected for their education. Then, declaring original human thinking to be evil, he ordered Christians to reject all "illegitimate secret books" as "invention[s] of heretics," full of "evil teachings they have clearly created."[82]

What has made this letter most famous is what follows: Athanasius set out a list of sacred books that, he declared, Christians could keep, a list that turned out to be *the earliest known record we have of what would become—and remains to this day—the church's New Testament canon.* After listing the twenty-two books of the Old Testament, Athanasius added twenty-seven books he called the only "*genuine . . .* books of the new testament," adding that "these are the springs of salvation; *these alone* teach true piety."

At a time when Christian leaders throughout the empire were discussing which books should be regarded as their "Scriptures," Athanasius intended his list not only as a *canon*—that is, a standard of measurement—but one that he insisted was *unchangeable.* To emphasize that his canon must remain exactly as he wrote it, Athanasius concluded his list with a warning that ancient scribes often used to prevent anyone from changing what they wrote: "*Let no one add to (these words) or subtract anything from them.*" The biblical book of Deuteronomy repeats this formula to warn listeners not to alter any of "God's words,"[83] and John of Patmos had echoed these words as he ended his own book of prophecies.[84]

As we have seen, Athanasius concluded his own New Testament canon with that most controversial of books, John's Book of Revelation, although he knew that it had ignited heated arguments ever since John had written it three hundred years earlier—arguments still ongoing.[85] Had it not been for Athanasius, would Revelation be in the Bible? Christian leaders in earlier centuries—Justin, Irenaeus, Tertullian—had championed it; but when bishops and Christian leaders among Athanasius' contemporaries composed *their* lists of "canonical books," all others whose lists survive left out John's Book of Revelation—and often *only* this book. Around 350 C.E., for example, when Athanasius' younger contemporary Bishop Cyril of Jerusalem preached a famous sermon at the Church of the Holy Sepulcher, listing for newcomers "the New Testament books," Cyril named all of the books now in the New Testament *except* Revelation. When he finished his list, Cyril warned, "and whatever books are not read in the churches, *do not read them,* even by yourself." About fifteen years later, in 363, a council of bishops in Asia Minor drew up a list of "the canonical books of the New and Old Testament," which they decreed were the only ones to be read in church; and they, too, omitted only the Book of Revelation. When another of Athanasius' contemporaries, the famous theologian Gregory of Nazianzus, wrote up a canon list, he, too, left this book out, and finished his own list by declaring that "if there is anything besides these, *it is not among the genuine books.*" Still another of Athanasius' contemporaries, Bishop Amphilochius of Iconium, who also omitted John's Book of Revelation, concluded his own list with sharp criticism of competing canons: "This is *the least falsified canon* of the divinely inspired Scriptures."

Bishop Eusebius of Caesarea, in Palestine, who forty years earlier had sparred with Athanasius' mentor, Bishop Alexander, over the wording of the Nicene Creed and who later became a confidant of the emperor Constantine, shows in his enormously influential *History of the Church* how much controversy John's book had aroused. Eusebius acknowledges that at the time he was writing (c. 325–340), there was as yet no officially accepted list of "canonized" New Testament books. Yet Eusebius expresses so much ambivalence about the Book of Revelation that he actually places it both on the list of books he calls "universally accepted" *and* on the list of books he calls "illegitimate."[86] First, then, after listing twenty-two writings he says are "universally recognized" as "New Testament writings," Eusebius tentatively adds that "in addition to these, one may add, *if it really seems right*, the Revelation of John, about which we shall give the different opinions at the appropriate time." Later, when he lists the books he calls "illegitimate," including the Acts of Paul, the Revelation of Peter, and the Gospel to the Hebrews—*none* of which are now in the New Testament—Eusebius includes John's Book of Revelation as well, qualifying his inconsistency by repeating, "*if it seems right*, since, as I said, some reject [this book], while others count it among the recognized books."[87]

In a later volume of his *History*, Eusebius quotes extensively from the writings of Athanasius' famous predecessor Dionysius, whom he calls "the great bishop of Alexandria,"[88] who presided over the city during earlier persecutions (c. 233–265). Dionysius reports how he personally had debated with Egyptian Christians he regarded as literal-minded, since they read John's book as prophesying that Christ would reign for a thousand years *on earth*—a view that Justin and Irenaeus both shared. Dionysius dismisses this view as naive, and repeats what earlier critics had said: that the Book of Revelation was "unintelligible, irrational, and the title false . . . [that] it is not John's, and is not a revelation at all." Yet Dionysius cautiously adds that he does not share these negative views: "I take the view that the interpretation of the various sections is largely a mystery. . . . I do not understand it, but I suspect that some deeper meaning is hidden in the words."

Dionysius says he agrees that the author's name is John, "and I agree that it is written by a holy and inspired writer, but I am not prepared to admit that he was the apostle John, the son of Zebedee and the brother of James," who, he believes, wrote the Gospel of John. Noting many differences between the two writings, Dionysius concludes that the author of the Book of Revelation must have been a different John. He points out differences that literary critics have noted ever since; for example, that John of Patmos often mentions his own name but never claims to be an apostle; that the tone of his writing, the style, and the language, which is "not really Greek" but uses "barbarous idioms," are distinctly different from those of the fourth gospel. Yet Dionysius concludes by saying that "I have not said these things to pour scorn upon [the author of Revelation]—do not imagine that!—but only to show how different the two books are."[89]

Given such a controversial history, why did Athanasius choose to place the Book of Revelation as the capstone of his New Testament canon? Although we have no simple answer, several suggestions emerge from what we know of its history and its use to this day. Many readers of the Christian Bible today say that its placement seems right, since, just as the Book of Genesis, which begins "in the beginning," opens the Hebrew Bible, so John's Book of Revelation closes the Christian Bible with his visions of the end of time, when the "new Jerusalem" descends from heaven to inaugurate the long-delayed kingdom of God.

Yet while Athanasius ended his list with Revelation, we do not know how his contemporaries placed it. And although Christians usually copied their sacred books into codices, some copied Revelation onto rolls, like an ordinary text. If we can clear our minds of its traditional identification with an apostle, we might see other reasons that Athanasius included it. In the first place, Athanasius surely noted that Revelation is the only book in *any* New Testament collection that claims that its own writings are divinely inspired prophecy. And, as noted above, John concludes his prophecies by adding the scribal formula meant to prevent anyone from adding to or subtracting from "God's words"—a formula to which John adds threats and promises that, he says, God will deliver:

> I warn everyone who hears the words of the prophecy of this book: if anyone adds to them, God will add to that person the plagues described in this book; if anyone takes away from the words of the book of this prophecy, God will take away that person's share in the tree of life and the holy city described in this book.[90]

Directly after Athanasius lists in his letter the books he calls "recognized," he adds his own solemn warning—as if it applied not only to John's prophecies but also to *his* list of "canonized" books. By concluding his canon with the Book of Revelation, which, in turn, closes with this warning against adding or subtracting anything, Athanasius encouraged Christians to read these words as countless believers have read them ever since. And because Athanasius believed that Jesus' disciple John wrote the Book of Revelation, he apparently took these words to mean that John, or even God himself, whose spirit inspired John, endorsed his canon, sealing what the bishop intended—and successfully campaigned to have become—the *fixed canon* of the New Testament.

Even more important, perhaps, is how Athanasius reinterpreted John's visions of cosmic war to apply to the battle that he
himself fought for more than forty-five years—the battle to establish what he regarded as "orthodox Christianity" against heresy.
Following the precedent set by Dionysius, his predecessor as
bishop of Alexandria, who advised that Revelation not be taken
literally, Athanasius, as we have seen, interpreted "the beast" not
as *Rome* but as *demonically deceived Christians* who unwittingly
"war against Christ," and he interpreted Babylon, the "great
whore," as none other than *heresy* personified.[91] In this way Athanasius succeeded in neutralizing any embarrassing indictment of
Rome while reinterpreting John's book in ways relevant to his own
time, for those living in a *Christianized* empire.

Furthermore, having fought so long against Christians whom
he called *maniacs* and *Satan's disciples*, Athanasius approved the
way John's prophecies move swiftly toward the climactic vision of
the last judgment. For John says that, after the sea, death, and
Hades give up "all the dead that were in them," everyone—the
dead and the living—shall stand before God's throne on that
"great and terrible day." Then the damned shall be cast into the
lake of fire as the new Jerusalem descends from heaven to earth to
receive the saved to dwell in glory, where God shall "wipe every
tear from their eyes."[92] Like Irenaeus, Athanasius interprets Revelation's cosmic war as a vivid picture of his own crusade against
heretics and reads John's visions as sharp warnings to Christian
dissidents: God is about to divide the saved from the damned—
which now means dividing the "orthodox" from "heretics."[93]

Since John's visions allow no neutral place to stand, Athanasius' reading suggests that what makes the difference between

heaven and hell is whether one believes in Jesus as "essentially the same being" as God, as the Nicene Creed prescribes, or rejects the "truth necessary for salvation" and so falls into everlasting fire, to be "tormented day and night, forever and ever."[94] By offering this interpretation of Revelation, Athanasius set an influential trend—one adopted by other Christians ever since, from Martin Luther and his Catholic critics to clashing Christian groups to this day. From more than a thousand years after that time, many Christians throughout the world painted vivid images of that last judgment on the back walls of their churches—from the humblest village church to the Vatican's Sistine Chapel, painted by Michelangelo—to serve as a final warning to those departing from worship.

Yet in that famous Easter letter in 367, Athanasius goes on to say that even establishing a fixed New Testament "canon" is not enough. Because he has heard that "the heretics" boast "about the books they call 'apocryphal,'" Athanasius orders that no one is to discuss or teach, much less read, what he calls the "empty and polluted" books written and revered by people "who do not seek what benefits the church."[95] As David Brakke points out, Athanasius singles out for special censure the apocalypses attributed to Moses, Isaiah, and Enoch, which he says are "filled with myths."[96] Thus he sought to censor the "secret books" that Christians apparently were reading, whether in private groups scattered in cities and towns along the Nile or in communal devotions.

We do not know exactly what happened in response to Athanasius' letter. What we do know is that, whether in response to this letter or to later denunciations of writings associated with

Origen, some time after Theodore ordered the bishop's letter to be copied onto the monastery wall at Nag Hammadi, someone— perhaps monks resisting the bishop's order—took more than fifty sacred writings, including gospels and secret "revelations," packed and carefully sealed them into a six-foot jar, and buried them for safekeeping near the cliff where they were discovered nearly fifteen hundred years later, in 1945, and came to be known as the Gnostic gospels.

One final note: as early as 315, the emperor Constantine took John's vision of Christ's victory over the dragon as an emblem of his rule. Constantine emblazoned this image in the most conspicuous public places, apparently to show that he, as Roman emperor, far from embodying "the beast," was now Christ's agent, who destroys all evil power. The emperor's friend and historian, Bishop Eusebius of Caesarea, describes having seen the "victorious trophy" that Constantine commissioned and "displayed on a very high panel placed before the entrance to the palace for everyone to see, showing in the picture the Savior's sign placed above his own head." So, Eusebius says, the emperor, adapting the visions of the prophets Isaiah and John of Patmos,

> showed to all . . . the dragon under his own feet and those of his sons, pierced through the middle of the body with a javelin, and thrust down in the depths of the sea. . . .
>
> In this way he indicated the invisible enemy of the human race, whom he showed also to have departed to the depths of destruction by the power of the Savior's trophy which was set up over his head.[97]

To display this image to his subjects in distant regions, Constantine ordered it struck on coins minted during his reign and circulated throughout the eastern empire. For after those crucial nights of battle and victory in October 312, when the energetic young emperor defeated and killed his rivals and ended persecution, he understood that he ruled through the power of Christ, having vanquished the dragon, whose evil power he now saw embodied in a far wider range of enemies. Eusebius says that for Constantine, the dragon represented not only the devil—"the invisible enemy of the human race"—but also Licinius, who initially reigned with him as co-regent and whom he later killed as a rival. Constantine wrote in a letter to Eusebius that he had restored "liberty to the human race" after he drove "*that dragon*" out of public administration."[98]

Taking cues from bishops Eusebius and Athanasius, Constantine also saw the "evil one" stirring up trouble among Christians. When he heard that bitter disputes had broken out among Christians in Africa around 317, Eusebius reported that

> he treated what was being done as ridiculous, and said he understood the provocation of the Evil One; that these people were either out of their minds, or goaded to frenzy by the evil demon.[99]

A few years later, when Constantine sought to defuse the quarrel between Arius and Bishop Alexander, he wrote a solemn, careful, and conciliatory letter to rebuke them both for "sparring like juveniles"[100] and to warn them to not succumb to "diabolic temptations," since the Evil One, the "common enemy of the whole world," often attacks from within, having "set his own lawless will against your holy synods."[101] When Constantine convened the council of Nicea to resolve their dispute, he opened by exhorting the assembled bishops "not to let the malicious demon encompass the divine law with blasphemies." A few years later, when he ordered that all the meeting places of "heretics" be confiscated and turned over to Catholic bishops, Eusebius says that he had "decided that certain people had to be eliminated from humanity like a poison," since they infect "the whole world" with "great evil." Finally, Constantine would include Jews among the horde of evildoers he felt called upon to vanquish, since he saw them as "killers of the prophets, and the murderers of the Lord."[102]

Nearly forty years after Constantine's death, Athanasius came toward the end of his own long crusade and died in May 373. To a remarkable extent, he had succeeded in his triple-pronged agenda mandating *creed*, *clergy*, and *canon*. Having been bishop for more than forty-five years (although he had spent seventeen of them in exile), he and his allies were able to require many monks, as well as other Christians, to accept the Nicene Creed as, indeed, the "truth necessary for salvation." He also had enormously extended the authority, resources, and prestige of the Catholic clergy, having brought many churches and monasteries under their supervision. Finally, he also had persuaded many Christians to accept his version of the canon as the only "authorized" scriptures of the New Testament.

This brief sketch of its history may help us see how the Book of Revelation came to be placed in the New Testament canon and enshrined in the Christian Roman Empire, but it does not answer a much larger question: How has this mysterious book of prophecies continued to speak to people thousands of years later, even now? Although to fully answer this question would require another book—or many books!—we turn to it in our conclusion.

Conclusion

The Book of Revelation reads as if John had wrapped up all our worst fears—fears of violence, plague, wild animals, unimaginable horrors emerging from the abyss below the earth, lightning, thunder, hail, earthquakes, erupting volcanoes, and the atrocities of torture and war—into one gigantic nightmare. Yet instead of ending in total destruction, his visions finally open to the new Jerusalem—a glorious city filled with light. John's visions of dragons, monsters, mothers, and whores speak less to our head than to our heart: like nightmares and dreams, they speak to what we fear, and what we hope.

Christian leaders have understood the uses of fear and hope from the time that Justin "the philosopher" threatened Roman emperors with hellfire and courageously defied the judge who ordered him beheaded by declaring that God would raise him back to life. Thus John's visions speak to what one historian calls the Christian movement's most powerful catalyst—the conviction that death is not simply annihilation. For after Jesus' earliest followers first said they had seen him alive after his death, many proclaimed that everyone, after death, would be raised to new life. But John's visions go further, as he vividly imagines *how* one might live after death—and what this means for how we live now.

John himself faithfully reproduces Jewish tradition that speaks of God judging people "according to their works,"[1] but his visions open up a far wider range of interpretations than, for example, Jesus' parable of divine judgment. For as Matthew tells it, that parable turns on specific deeds. The Son of Man invites into God's kingdom those he calls blessed,

> for I was hungry and you gave me food; I was thirsty and you gave me something to drink; I was a stranger and you welcomed me; I was naked, and you gave me clothing; I was sick and you took care of me; I was in prison and you visited me.[2]

When his hearers protest that they have never seen him in such straits, he replies, "Whenever you did it to the least of these members of my family, you did it to me." Shut out from God's kingdom are those who withhold care and compassion from those in need.

By contrast, John of Patmos conjures cosmic war, good fighting evil until Christ crushes the dragon, through visions that can be plugged into almost any conflict. Because John more often defines "evildoers" with degrading epithets—"cowards, the faithless, abominable, filthy . . . and all liars"[3]—than with specific deeds, nearly anyone might claim to be on God's side, fighting "evildoers." Throughout the ages, John of Patmos' visions have fortified religious anger like his own, the anger of those who suffer oppression and long for retaliation against those who torture and kill their people. Yet those who torture and kill in God's name often cast themselves into the same drama, seeing themselves not as the "murderers" John denounces but as God's servants delivering divine judgment.

From the end of the second century to the fourth, as the movement increasingly developed institutional structures, some Christian leaders began to divide "the saved" from "the damned" less in terms of how they act than whether they accept a certain set of doctrines and participate—or don't—in specific religious communities. Those who followed Athanasius' ingenious reinterpretation of "whore" and "beast" as *Christian* enemies often came to identify "orthodox" believers alone as the saved, while consigning everyone who stood outside the Catholic communion—pagans, Jews, "infidels," along with any Christians they called heretics—to outer darkness, both in this world and the next.

Those adopting these lines of interpretation could appreciate how John's apocalyptic visions helped create coherence among all who identified as Catholic Christians and to establish a common bulwark against all whom they saw as outsiders. Ever since, Christians have adapted his visions to changing times, reading their own social, political, and religious conflict into the cosmic war he so powerfully evokes. Perhaps most startling is how Constantine invoked John's vision of Christ's victory over Rome to endorse his own imperial rule. More than a thousand years later, Lutherans published Lucas Cranach's pictures of the pope as the whore of Babylon in one of the first Lutheran Bibles, while an early Catholic biographer retaliated by depicting Luther, on the frontispiece, as the seven-headed beast. During the catastrophic times of the American Civil War, Confederate loyalists portrayed Lincoln being strangled by the great dragon that is the Union, while those on the Union side took as their war anthem "Battle Hymn of the Republic," which weaves Jeremiah's and John's prophecies in to

that war, now seen as the Great Tribulation that precedes God's
final judgment:

> Mine eyes have seen the glory of the coming of the Lord;
> He is trampling out the vintage where the grapes of wrath
>   are stored;
> He hath loosed the fateful lightning of His terrible, swift
>   sword;
> Our God is marching on.

We need not rehearse the history of religious violence—from cru-
saders fighting "infidels" and inquisitors torturing and killing
Jews to save their immortal souls, to Catholics and Protestants
fighting religious wars from the sixteenth century on, or Christian groups engaged in vigilante violence to the present time, or
the wartime rhetoric of world leaders—to realize how often those
who wield power and see themselves standing on God's side
against Satan's have sought to force "God's enemies" to submit or
be killed. Such apocalyptic fervor, whether engaged in by Christians or Muslims, allows no neutral ground between God's kingdom and the lake of fire, and no room for compromise, much less
for human—or humane—interaction.

During the years in which Christians debated whether to
place the Book of Revelation into the church's definitive canon,
other writers inspired by John of Patmos revised and amplified
his warnings of the coming judgment. The scholar David Frankfurter has shown how the anonymous author of the Revelation of
Elijah, writing in Egypt circa 250, updated "the signs of the time"
to warn his contemporaries of God's coming judgment.[4] The

Revelation of Paul, too, sharply separated the saved from the damned, taking special care to show how the divine judge would tailor hell's tortures to fit each sinner's crime,[5] as its author contributed to a stream that eventually would include Dante's *Inferno* and Milton's *Paradise Lost,* and paintings by artists as diverse as Michelangelo and Bosch, William Blake and Picasso, as well as countless films and video games being produced to this day.

Yet John's Book of Revelation appeals not only to fear but also to hope. As John tells how the chaotic events of the world are finally set right by divine judgment, those who engage his visions often see them offering meaning—moral meaning—in times of suffering or apparently random catastrophe. Many poets, artists, and preachers who engage these prophecies claim to have found in them the promise, famously repeated by Martin Luther King Jr., that "the arc of the moral universe is long, but it bends toward justice."[6]

Finally, too, this worst of all nightmares ends not in terror but in a glorious new world, radiant with the light of God's presence, flowing with the water of life, abounding in joy and delight. Whether one sees in John's visions the destruction of the whole world or the dark tunnel that propels each of us toward our own death, his final vision suggests that even after the worst we can imagine has happened, we may find the astonishing gift of new life. Whether one shares that conviction, few readers miss seeing how these visions offer consolation and that most necessary of divine gifts—hope.

But we have seen that the story of this book moves beyond its own pages to include the church leaders who made it the final book in the New Testament canon, which they then declared closed, and scriptural revelation complete. After Athanasius sought to censor all *other* "revelations" and to silence all whose views differed from the orthodox consensus, his successors worked hard to make sure that Christians could not read "any books except the common catholic books."[7]

Orthodox Christians acknowledge that some revelation may occur even now, but since most accept as genuine only what agrees with the traditional consensus, those who speak for minority—or original—views are often excluded.

Left out are the visions that lift their hearers beyond apocalyptic polarities to see the human race as a whole—and, for that matter, to see each one of us as a whole, having the capacity for both cruelty and compassion. Those who championed John's Revelation finally succeeded in obliterating visions associated with Origen, the "father of the church" posthumously condemned as a heretic some three hundred years after his death, who envisioned animals, stars, and stones, as well as humans, demons, and angels, sharing a common origin and destiny. Writings not directly connected with Origen, like The Secret Revelation of John, the Gospel of Truth, and Thunder, Perfect Mind, also speak of the kinship of all beings with one another and with God. Living in an increasingly interconnected world, we need such universal visions more than ever. Recovering such lost and silenced voices, even when we don't accept everything they say, reminds us that even our clearest insights are more like glimpses "seen through a glass darkly"[8] than maps of complete and indelible truth.

Many of these secret writings, as we've seen, picture "the living Jesus" inviting questions, inquiry, and discussions about meaning—unlike Tertullian when he complains that "questions make people heretics" and demands that his hearers stop asking questions and simply accept the "rule of faith."[9] And unlike those who insist that they already have all the answers they'll ever need, these sources invite us to recognize our own truths, to find our own voice, and to seek revelation not only past, but ongoing.

NOTES

CHAPTER ONE: John's Revelation:
Challenging the Evil Empire, Rome

1 Ernest L. Tuveson, *Redeemer Nation: The Idea of America's Millennial Role* (Chicago: University of Chicago Press, 1968). For a recent and challenging view, see Kathryn Gin, *Damned Nation: The Concept of Hell in American Life, 1775–1865* (New York: Oxford University Press, forthcoming, 2012). I am grateful to the Rev. Tony Campolo for pointing out, in his letter of March 21, 2011, that many Evangelical Christians today see in the Book of Revelation "a description of what is going on in America" and, especially in Revelation 18 and 19, an indictment of political and economic systems built on military power and consumerism.

2 Note Elisabeth Schüssler Fiorenza's perceptive discussion of several strategies often used for reading this book, in her *Revelation: Vision of a Just World*, ed. G. Krodel (Minneapolis: Fortress Press, 1991), "Reading Revelation in and from the Margins," 6–20, as well as 117ff. See also *The Book of Revelation: Justice and Judgment*, 2nd ed. (Minneapolis: Fortress Press, 1998), especially her article "*Apocalypsis* and *Propheteia*: Revelation in the Context of Early Christian Prophecy," 133–158. See also Brian K. Blount, "The Witness of Active Resistance: The Ethics of Revelation in African American Perspective," in David Rhoads,

From Every People and Nation: The Book of Revelation in Intercultural Perspective (Minneapolis: Fortress Press, 2005), 1–27, and also his recently published commentary, *Revelation* (Louisville: John Knox Press, 2009).

3 Eusebius, *The History of the Church*, VII, 24.1–27; for discussion, see chapter 5, pages 162–163.

4 See the passage cited in note 3 for the fullest extant account of Dionysius' views on the Book of Revelation.

5 For an overview of the use of this book, including that by Luther and his critics, see, for example, Arthur W. Wainwright, *Mysterious Apocalypse: Interpreting the Book of Revelation* (New York: Wipf and Stock Publishers, 2001), 55ff; and Judith Kovacs and Christopher Rowland, *Revelation: The Apocalypse of Jesus Christ* (Madden, MA: Blackwell Publishing, 2004), 19–20, 44–45.

6 The term as used here is not intended to indicate genre. For although the term "apocalypse" is used in the Nag Hammadi library more often than terms like "gospel" or "apocryphon," various terms are used for writings that claim to offer "revelation," as David Frankfurter notes in his article "The Legacy of Jewish Apocalypses in Early Christianity: Regional Trajectories," in James VanderKam and William Adler, eds., *The Jewish Heritage in Early Christianity* (Assen, Netherlands: Van Gorum & Comp, 1996), 135, 156. Noted scholar of early Christian apocalyptic literature Brian E. Daley, S.J., points out that while "the Nag Hammadi collection . . . contains a number of texts labeled 'apocalypses' . . . for the most part these revelation-discourses have little literary connection with the traditional apocalyptic form," in "Faithful and True: Early Christian Apocalyptic and the Person of Christ," in Robert J. Daly, S.J., *Apocalyptic Thought in Early Christianity* (Grand Rapids, MI: Baker Academic, 2009), 114. Many scholars would agree with him that these are "partial heirs of the apocalyptic tradition,

rather than its authentic representatives," 115. Most of those found at Nag Hammadi do not focus primarily upon apocalyptic eschatology, nor do they conform to the attempt to define the genre set forth in John J. Collins' influential work, exemplified in "The Genre Apocalypse in Hellenistic Judaism," in *Apocalypticism in the Mediterranean World and the Near East: Proceedings of the International Colloquium in Apocalypticism, Uppsala,* ed. David Hellholm (Tübingen, Germany: Mohr Siebeck, 1983), 531–548.

7 Revelation 1:10; for discussion of this phrase (and, indeed, of any throughout the entire book), see David Aune, *Revelation 1–5, Word Biblical Commentary,* vol. 52, A, B, C (Nashville, TN: Thomas Nelson Publishers, 1997), vol. 52A, 82–83.

8 Revelation 1:12–16.

9 Revelation 4:1.

10 Revelation 1:19, now about to be revealed through the opening of the sealed scroll of Revelation 5.

11 Revelation 6:4. For John's vision of all the horsemen, see 6:2–8.

12 Revelation 6:10.

13 Revelation 9:1–3.

14 Revelation 9:7–11.

15 Revelation 12:1–6. Since the earliest commentators, Christians often have interpreted her as Mary, since she is characterized as mother of the messiah or else as the church. Others, likely including John himself, inspired by the image that the prophet Isaiah offers in Isaiah 26:17–27:1, apparently thought of her as the nation of Israel as potentially pregnant with the messiah, have seen her as an image of Israel. The reader need not choose one of these interpretations to the exclusion of others. Note, for example, how John J. Collins, in his influential book *The Apocalyptic Imagination: An Introduction to the Jewish Matrix of Christianity* (New York: Crossroad Publishing, 1984), 11ff, characterizes

apocalyptic images as "multivalent," that is, capable of suggesting more than one meaning—often a cluster of related meanings.

16 For an excellent discussion, see Neil Forsyth, *The Old Enemy: Satan and the Combat Myth* (Princeton, NJ: Princeton University Press, 1987), 248–257, especially 252: "in chapter 12 . . . is the only explicit reference in the New Testament to a war in heaven." For an extensive and influential discussion of the background of these traditions, see Adela Yarbro Collins, *The Combat Myth in the Book of Revelation* (Missoula, MT: Scholars Press, 1976).

17 Revelation 12:17.

18 For John's description of the beasts, see Revelation 13:1–18. Regarding the number of the beast, some ancient manuscripts give the name of the beast as the number 616, as Irenaeus notes; e.g. P. Oxy. LXVI 4499. On this topic as a text-critical issue, see David C. Parker, *An Introduction to the New Testament Manuscripts and Their Texts* (Cambridge, UK: Cambridge University Press, 2008), 242–244.

19 Revelation 16:13. For John's account of the seven angels who dispense God's wrath, see 15:5–16:21.

20 Revelation 1:2. Tina Pippin, among others, discusses John's use of feminine images such as the "woman clothed with the sun," Jerusalem, the virgin bride, and the whore of Babylon; see "The Heroine and the Whore: Fantasy and the Female in the Apocalypse of John," *Semeia 60: Fantasy and the Bible* (1991), 67–82. See response by Elisabeth Schüssler Fiorenza, *The Book of Revelation: Justice and Judgment*, 217–226. For a major critique of apocalyptic thinking, see Catherine Keller, *Apocalypse Now and Then: A Feminist Guide to the End of the World* (Boston: Beacon Press, 1996).

21 Revelation 19:11–16.

22 Revelation 19:17–18.

23 Revelation 21:8.

24 Scholars have long debated the precise dating of John's writing, the most probable dates being either around 68 C.E. or 90–96 C.E. Although we cannot be certain of the date, I find the latter more plausible. For a short discussion of the factors to consider, see Adela Yarbro Collins, *Crisis and Catharsis: The Power of the Apocalypse* (Philadelphia: Westminster Press, 1984), 54–83. For another carefully considered view of composite composition, see Aune, *Revelation 1–5, vol.* 52A, lvi–lxx.

25 For the classic account of this war, see Josephus, *The Jewish War,* available in an English translation by G. A. Williamson (St. Ives Place, UK: Penguin, 1981).

26 Revelation 1:2. While John's account has often suggested to his readers that he was forcibly exiled, perhaps as a prisoner, recent commentators have challenged that claim; see, for example, the discussion by Yarbro Collins in *Crisis and Catharsis,* especially 25–53; Aune, *Revelation 1–5,* vol. 52A, xlvii–xc; the important contribution by Leonard L. Thompson, *The Book of Revelation: Apocalypse and Empire* (New York: Oxford University Press, 1991); and Paul Duff's careful account "Was There a Crisis Behind Revelation? An Introduction to the Problem," in *Who Rides the Beast? Prophecy and the Rhetoric of Crisis in the Churches of the Apocalypse* (Oxford: Oxford University Press, 2001), 3–16, 17–82.

27 See Bruce Malina, *On the Genre and Message of Revelation: Star Visions and Sky Journeys* (Peabody, MA: Hendrickson, 1995), an interesting book (although one that, as a colleague notes, might "overplay the evidence") about what John might have seen of constellations.

28 See Mark 6:27–30 (and parallels), which suggests that Jesus allowed his disciples to infer this designation and tacitly accepted it.

29 Revelation 19:16.

30 Mark 13:1–2.

31 Did Jesus actually predict the destruction of the temple? Many scholars maintain that these prophecies were retrojected into his teaching by his followers after that shocking event in 70 c.e., apparently on the assumption that "Jesus could not have known that this would happen." In a forthcoming article, I show why I find this view unpersuasive. Here's a quick summary: First, because other prophets had made similar predictions before its destruction, as did Jesus ben Ananias, in the early 60s; second, because Mark's account is contradictory, claiming that Jesus was accused of having threatened to destroy the temple—an accusation Mark insists is entirely false (Mark 14:56–58); third, when Mark admits that Jesus did prophesy the temple's destruction (Mark 13:1–2), the account of his words does not accord with what actually happened, as one would tend to expect with retrojected prophecy (there are stones standing upon others— quite a few of them, to this day).

32 Mark 9:1, 13:30.

33 See Mark 13:7–19; see also 13:1–30; see also parallels in Luke 21:5–28 and Matthew 24:1–31.

34 Mark 13:29–30. See Brian Daley's book *The Hope of the Early Church: A Handbook of Patristic Eschatology* (New York: Cambridge University Press, 1991), for an overview of the evidence for the view that early Christian preaching was primarily apocalyptic, with which many scholars, including myself, agree.

35 For discussion, see the important book by Simon R. F. Price, *Rituals and Power: The Roman Imperial Cult in Asia Minor* (Cambridge, UK: Cambridge University Press, 1984), especially "Part II: The Evocations of Imperial Rituals," 133–274.

36 The following discussion is owed especially to the outstanding study by Steven J. Friesen, *Imperial Cults and the Apocalypse of*

John: Reading Revelation in the Ruins (Oxford: Oxford University Press, 2001).

37 See the discussion by Friesen, *Imperial Cults*, 90–95.

38 Price, *Rituals and Power*, especially 1–77.

39 See Gaius Suetonius, "Divus Julius" and "Divus Augustus," *The Twelve Caesars*, trans. Robert Graves, rev. ed. (London: Penguin, 2007), 1–103; Plutarch, *Lives*, trans. Arthur H. Clough (New York: Modern Library, 2001), vol. II: "Anthony," 481–534.

40 Psalm 96:5 (95:5 in the Septuagint), translated from the original Hebrew into Greek, could suggest this reading. (ὅτι πάντες οἱ θεοὶ τῶν ἐθνῶν δαιμόνια.)

41 In his fine study of visions in Jewish medieval sources, Elliot Wolfson comments that "one may presume" that these "were induced by specific visionary practices, though the records of these visions were often expressed in conventional imagery drawn from the theophanic traditions in Hebrew Scriptures," in *Through a Speculum That Shines: Vision and Imagination in Medieval Jewish Mysticism* (Princeton, NJ: Princeton University Press, 1994), 28. For a discussion of such practices, see Dan Merkur, "The Visionary Practices of Jewish Apocalypticists," in *Psychoanalytic Study of Society* 14 (1989): 119–148.

42 Revelation 1:12–17. John's vision seems to combine features that Daniel uses to describe the Ancient of Days in the vision he relates in Daniel 7:9b and the angelic presence he describes in 10:5–9.

43 Revelation 3:10.

44 Ezekiel 1:26–28.

45 Revelation 5:2.

46 Revelation 5:5.

47 For an intriguing discussion on the juxtaposition of the lion/lamb images, see Aune, *Revelation 1–5*, vol. 52A: 332–338; 349–355, and Friesen, *Imperial Cults*, especially part II,

"Revelation, Resistance," and "The Authority of the Lamb," 135, 197–209.

48 Some of Jesus' earliest followers, noting the proximity of his crucifixion and Passover, made this connection explicit, as did Paul of Tarsus, saying that "Christ, our Passover [lamb] has been sacrificed for us" (I Corinthians 5:7b), and the author of the Gospel of John, who actually narrates the account of Jesus' death as if it had coincided with the slaughter of the Passover lambs (John 19:14ff).

49 Revelation 6:1–2. For discussion of what this means in the context of John's prophecy, see Pierre Prigent, *Commentary on the Apocalypse of St. John*, trans. W. Pradels (Tübingen, Germany: Mohr Siebeck, 2001), 262f; Duff, *Who Rides the Beast?* 83–125; Pagels, "The Social History of Satan, Part III: John of Patmos and Ignatius of Antioch—Contrasting Visions of 'God's People,'" *Harvard Theological Review* 99.4 (2006): 487–505.

50 John Marshall interprets such evidence to suggest that John wrote during—or directly after—this intense time of war and assassination; see *Parables of War: Reading John's Jewish Apocalypse* (Waterloo, Ontario: Wilfred Laurier Press, 2001).

51 Revelation 6:16–17.

52 Revelation 7:13–17.

53 Historian Adela Yarbro Collins helpfully reminded me in a letter that John apparently took the ten plagues against the Egyptians in Exodus as his model for Revelation 8:8–9.

54 Revelation 8:8–9.

55 Revelation 10:1–6.

56 Revelation 11:15.

57 Revelation 12:1–4.

58 Neil Forsythe points out that this "is the only explicit reference in the New Testament to a war in heaven, and so the key text for the war in later tradition," *The Old Enemy*, 252; while, as my colleague

Martha Himmelfarb reminds me, the prophet Daniel refers to war between the angels of the various nations, including Persia and Israel. See also the work of Adela Yarbro Collins and, more recently, Pagels, "The Social History of Satan, Part III," 487–494.

59 Revelation 12:7–9.

60 Revelation 12:18–13:4.

61 *Enuma Elish*, 137.

62 Psalm 74:12–14.

63 For example, see Yarbro Collins, *The Combat Myth in the Book of Revelation*.

64 Genesis 1:1–2.

65 Genesis 1:21.

66 Much of this discussion is owed to the brilliant analysis of the Genesis accounts by Jon D. Levenson, *Creation and the Persistence of Evil: The Jewish Drama of Divine Omnipotence* (Princeton, NJ: Princeton University Press, 1994). Although later readers often took these dragons as images of evil, Richard Clifford, S.J., suggests that such images originally referred simply to the hostile forces that the king had to defeat in order to become or remain king; see his article "The Roots of Apocalypticism in Near Eastern Myth," in *The Encyclopedia of Apocalypticism*, vol. 1, *The Origins of Apocalypticism in Judaism and Christianity*, eds. John J. Collins, Stephen Stein, and Bernard McGinn (New York: Continuum Press, 2000), 3–38. (I owe this reference to Professor Adela Yarbro Collins.)

67 Psalm 74: 3b–7.

68 Jeremiah 51:34–35.

69 Ezekiel 32:2–4.

70 Ezekiel 29:3–5, 29:12.

71 More precisely put, scholars refer this way to this section of the prophetic text.

72 Isaiah 51:9–10.

73 Isaiah 27:1.

74 Isaiah 26:16–17.

75 I appreciate Adela Yarbro Collins' comment that Isaiah 26:16–17 "does not seem to use the figure of a woman in labor with reference to the messiah." Yet John of Patmos seems to interpret the passage in that way to adapt it to his own view of Jesus of Nazareth as Israel's messiah, here pictured as the child who escapes to heaven.

76 Revelation 12:1–3.

77 Revelation 12:17.

78 Daniel 7:19–20; see below, note 81.

79 Daniel 8:15, 8:27.

80 Daniel 7:14.

81 Revelation 13:2. As Adela Yarbro Collins points out, while the beasts of Daniel 7 represent the Babylonian, Median, Persian, and Hellenistic empires, Daniel's first-century interpreters, including John of Patmos, Josephus, and Salathiel, the author of the Fourth Book of Ezra, later interpreted the fourth kingdom as the one with which they had to contend—Rome.

82 For an overview of some recent discussion, see, for example, Yarbro Collins, *Crisis and Catharsis*, 58–64.

83 Revelation 13:3, 13:14. See Hans-Josef Klauk, "Do They Never Come Back? *Nero Redivivus* and the *Revelation of John*," in *Catholic Biblical Quarterly* I:63 (2001): 683–698.

84 Suetonius, "Nero," *The Twelve Caesars*, 207–254.

85 Revelation 15:18.

86 Revelation 8:8–9. For references and discussion, see David Aune, *Revelation 6–16*, *Word Biblical Commentary*, vol. 52B (Nashville, TN: Thomas Nelson, 1988), 519–520.

87 Professor Paul Duff and others suggest that rather than hiding his language for this reason, John was self-consciously using the genre "apocalypse," which, as he understood it, "called for

such symbolic language." Professor Duff kindly referred me back to Leonard Thompson's analysis in *The Book of Revelation: Apocalypse and Empire* (New York: Oxford University Press, 1990), 191–197.

88 Revelation 10:6.

89 For this term and for his influential discussion of apocalyptic language, see Collins, *The Apocalyptic Imagination*, cited in note 15 of this chapter.

90 Although Richard Clifford denies that the imagery of Revelation, as well as that of its predecessors and sources, originally did not refer to evil versus good, as later interpreters often assume (see his article cited in note 66 of this chapter), what interests me here is the interpretive tradition for which this reading has become axiomatic.

CHAPTER TWO: Visions of Heaven and Hell:
From Ezekiel and John of Patmos to Paul

Please note: Scholars and students are advised to consult the more technical version of the discussion presented here in my 2006 article "The Social History of Satan, Part III: John of Patmos and Ignatius of Antioch—Contrasting Visions of 'God's People,'" *Harvard Theological Review* 99.4 (2006).

1 On the religious wars of Europe, see Andrew Cunningham and Ole P. Grell, *The Four Horsemen of the Apocalypse: Religion, War, Famine, and Death in Reformation Europe* (Cambridge, UK: Cambridge University Press, 2000); Katherine B. Firth, *The Apocalyptic Tradition in Reformation Britain 1530–1645* (Oxford, UK: Oxford University Press, 1979);

2 Terrie D. Aamodt, *Righteous Armies, Holy Cause: Apocalyptic Imagery and the Civil War* (Macon, GA: Mercer University Press, 2002).

3 For an overview and many examples, see, for example, Richard Steigmann-Gall, *The Holy Reich: Nazi Conceptions of Christianity, 1919–1945,* (Cambridge, UK: Cambridge University Press, 2003); see also the recent and important book by Susannah Heschel, *The Aryan Jesus: Christian Theologians and the Bible in Nazi Germany* (Princeton, NJ: Princeton University Press, 2008).

4 William Blake, *The Everlasting Gospel,* a.13–14.

5 Revelation 2:20.

6 See chapter 1, note 6, for discussions that show that these other books of revelation do not constitute a single literary genre, nor are they all primarily concerned with apocalyptic eschatology; for an introductory discussion of these sources, see Pagels, *The Gnostic Gospels* (New York: Random House, 1979).

7 Isaiah 6:1–3.

8 Ezekiel 1:1–2.

9 Ezekiel 1:15–25.

10 Exodus 33:20. For a brilliant discussion of how Jewish visionaries later claimed to "see" the God whom some biblical sources say cannot be seen, see Wolfson, *Through a Speculum That Shines,* especially 13–67; and Gerhard von Rad, *The Message of the Prophets,* trans. D.M.G. Stalker (London: SCM Press, 1965), 33–49.

11 Ezekiel 1: 26–28. See also chapter 1, page 4.

12 See the influential discussion of early Jewish mysticism by Peter Schäfer in *The Hidden and Manifest God: Some Major Themes in Early Jewish Mysticism,* trans. Aubrey Pomerance (Albany: SUNY Press, 1992).

13 Revelation 1:9b–10, 4:2.

14 For this part of the throne-room vision, see Revelation 4:2–8.

15 Mark 1:9–11.

16 Revelation 1:17.

17 Acts 22:6–10; see also 9:3–6.

18 Galatians 1:16.

19 Galatians 1:12.

20 See Galatians 1:12–2:14. Hans D. Betz comments, "Paul himself admits that the delegation was sent to Jerusalem in order to get some kind of belated approval by the authorities for Paul's and Barnabas' gospel, that is, the gospel which was free from Torah and circumcision," in *Galatians: A Commentary on Paul's Letter to the Churches in Galatia* (Minneapolis: Fortress Press, 1979), 86.

21 For "super apostles," see 2 Corinthians 12:11.

22 2 Corinthians 12:1.

23 2 Corinthians 12:2–3.

24 2 Corinthians 12:4.

25 2 Corinthians 12:4.

26 Note that some prominent scholars of Revelation, including Elisabeth Schüssler Fiorenza, place John *within* Pauline tradition; see, for example, Schüssler Fiorenza's "Apocalyptic and Gnosis in the Book of Revelation and Paul," *Journal of Biblical Literature* 92:4 (December 1973): 565–581; in *L'Apocalypse Johannique et l'Apocalyptique dans le Nouveau Testament*, ed. Jan Lambrecht (Louvain, Belgium: Colloquium Biblicum Lovaniense, 1979), 105–128.

27 John echoes in Revelation 1:6 words said to have been dictated from God to Moses, addressing Israel, in Exodus 19:6.

28 Revelation 2:2.

29 Tertullian, *Prescription Against Heresies*, 36, in *Ante Nicene Fathers Library* 3 (Grand Rapids, MI: Eerdmans, 1951), 260.

30 John Gager, *Kingdom and Community: The Social World of Early Christianity* (Englewood Cliffs, NJ: Prentice Hall, 1975), 27; Yarbro Collins, *Crisis and Catharsis*, 84–110. See also Leonard L. Thompson's influential discussion of the historical sources on Domitian, during whose reign John is probably writing, in *The*

Book of Revelation; see also Prigent's perceptive review of recent discussion in his *Commentary on the Apocalypse of St. John,* 71–79.

31 Revelation 2:10, 2:13.

32 Revelation 2:10.

33 Genesis 12:2. See also Isaiah 60:3.

34 Acts 11:26. Other passages, like 14:1, say that Paul spoke in the synagogue so that "a great number of both Jews and Greeks became believers," as he mentions repeatedly throughout the entire book. See the incisive discussion by David Frankfurter, "Jews or Not? Reconstructing the 'Other' in Rev 2:9 and 3:9," *Harvard Theological Review* 94 (2001): 403–425. See also John Marshall's "Collateral Damage: Jesus and Jezebel in the Jewish War," eds. Shelley Matthews and E. Leigh Gibson, *Violence in the New Testament* (London: T&T Clark, 2005), 35–50.

35 Revelation 2:9, 3:9.

36 Revelation 2:9.

37 Revelation 2:13.

38 As Prigent observes in his *Commentary,* 73. When Prigent considers those against whom John polemicizes, however, he repeatedly interprets them as *heretics,* although this term never occurs in John's book, nor, so far as we can tell, in his vocabulary. Despite that, Prigent repeatedly states that "in each of these letters, *in a matter that is more or less apparent,* mention is made of heretics" (italics mine), 132. I find this inference by no means apparent.

39 See Prigent's discussion in his *Commentary,* 50–68.

40 On Philo, see his own writings, published in the Loeb Classical Library Series.

41 Revelation 2:13.

42 Revelation 2:14.

43 Revelation 2:20–23. Schüssler Fiorenza notes that "The expression *ta tekna autes* (2:23) characterizes Jezebel as the head of a

prophetic 'school,' circle, or 'house church.' . . . Being a child of someone means to belong to someone's fellowship or to be a disciple of someone. . . . Therefore we can assume that in Thyatira the prophetic circle of Jezebel rivaled the influence of John, who discredits this group because he considers its teachings to be false and dangerous for the Christian community," in *"Apocalypsis* and *Propheteia*: The Book of Revelation in the Context of Early Christian Prophecy," in *L'Apocalypse Johannique et l'Apocalyptique dans le Nouveau Testament*, 105–128; also published in *The Book of Revelation: Justice and Judgment* (Minneapolis: Fortress Press, 1998), 133–158.

44   I Kings 16:31, 19:1–2.

45   See, for example, Hosea 1–2:20; Isaiah 50:1.

46   For an informative discussion, see Duff, *Who Rides the Beast?* 51–55.

47   Acts 15:20, 15:29.

48   Revelation 2:20–22.

49   David Frankfurter, "Jews or Not?" 403–425. Duff, in his article "Wolf in Sheep's Clothing: Literary Opposition and Social Tension in the Revelation of John," emphasizes that John of Patmos "never directly accuses the addressees" of actually engaging in these "unclean" acts but "rather, he accuses them of tolerating those who do so," *Reading the Book of Revelation*, ed. David Barr (Atlanta: Society of Biblical Literature, 2003), 67.

50   Revelation 6:4ff; also 14:3–4.

51   For an intriguing discussion of the imagery of war, compared with that in the War of the Sons of Light Against the Sons of Darkness, see Richard Bauckham, "The Apocalypse as a Christian War Scroll," in *The Climax of Prophecy: Studies on the Book of Revelation* (London: T&T Clark, 1993), 210–237. Pierre Prigent sets forth a different view: that the "one hundred and forty four thousand" is "made up of all the baptized [Christians]"; see

his *Commentary*, 284. Prigent interprets the "seal" with which John says the angels seal these men as Christian baptism (285).

52 Eusebius, the Palestinian bishop (c. 318–330), apparently based this on his reading of descriptions that Philo wrote in his treatise *On the Contemplative Life*, 25. See Eusebius' *History of the Church*. Prigent comments that "the community at Qumran believed it was experiencing the eschatological salvation.... Naturally it awaits the decisive judgment in which God will eliminate injustice," in his *Commentary*, 25.

53 Josephus' most extensive discussion is found in *The Jewish War* II:8.119–160; see also *Jewish Antiquities* XIII:11, 2; XV:10, 5; XVII:13.3.

54 Revelation 13:16–17; see Yarbro Collins, *Crisis and Catharsis*, 124–127; Duff, *Who Rides the Beast?* 68–70.

55 Revelation 14:9–11.

56 Bauckham, *The Climax of Prophecy*, 210–237.

57 See discussion in Aune, *Revelation 1–5*, vol. 52A: 185–245; Schüssler Fiorenza, "*Apocalypsis* and *Propheteia*," 109; Yarbro Collins, *Crisis and Catharsis*, 34–50; and the extensive discussion by Duff, *Who Rides the Beast?* especially "The Actors: People and Parties Behind the *Book of Revelation*," 48–60, and "True and False Prophets: Binding 'Jezebel' to the Beast from the Earth," 113–125.

58 Many commentators have noticed this; see, for example, the discussion by Duff, *Who Rides the Beast?* 54–55. David Frankfurter, in his important article "Jews or Not?" incisively qualifies that those to whom John refers are "Pauline and neo-Pauline proselytes to the Jesus movement who were not, in John's eyes ... halakically pure enough to merit this term" (403). The suggestion made above is by no means original; more than 150 years ago, members of the Tübingen school made similar suggestions; see Gustav Volkmar, *Kommentar zur Offenbarung Johnannes*

(Zürich: Drell, 1862), 80–85, and Ferdinand C. Baur, *Vorlesungen über neutestamentliche Theologie* (Leipzig, Germany: L. W. Reisland, 1864). For more recent discussion, see Ulrich B. Müller, *Zur frühchristlichen Theologiegeschichte: Judenchristentum und Paulinismus in Kleinasien an der Wende vom ersten zum zweiten Jahrhundert n. Chr.* (Gütersloh, Germany: Düterslocher Veragshaus Mohn, 1976), and Akira Satake, *Die Gemeindeordnung in der Johannesapokalypse* (Neukirchen, Germany: WMANT, 21, 1966).

59 I Corinthians 8:4.

60 I Corinthians 8:9–13.

61 I Corinthians 7:12–14.

62 Acts 15:1–33. Paul's account agrees that his meeting with James and Peter concluded as they "gave me and Barnabas the right hand of fellowship" (Galatians 2:9); but Hans D. Betz, for example, sees this as a rather forced compromise on their part; see his discussion in *Galatians: A Commentary on Paul's Letters to the Churches in Galatia* (Minneapolis: Fortress Press, 1979), 86–101. (Note, too, Schliers' view, which Betz cites on page 87, note 282.)

63 Galatians 1:15; note Paul's entire account, from 1:6 to 2:14.

64 Galatians 2:1–2.

65 Galatians 2:11.

66 Galatians 2:12–22.

67 Galatians 1:5–6.

68 Galatians 1:8–9.

69 Revelation 3:12.

70 For a vivid and informative description of these groups, see Wayne A. Meeks, *The First Urban Christians: The Social World of the Apostle Paul* (New Haven, CT: Yale University Press, 1963).

71 Romans 6:3.

72 Revelation 3:9.

73 Revelation 2:9.

74 See, for example, Schüssler Fiorenza, "Apocalyptic and Gnosis in Revelation and Paul," in *The Book of Revelation: Justice and Judgment*, 107. Aune, in *Revelation 1–5*, vol. 52A, 163, notes that "Here it is important to realize that the term 'Jews' is used positively," yet he takes John to be denouncing "those [Jews] associated with the synagogues in Smyrna and Philadelphia." Yarbro Collins, *Crisis and Catharsis*, 85: "The name 'Jews' is denied to the Jewish community in Smyrna. There is no good reason to think here of Judaizers rather than actual Jews of the local synagogues." See also the discussion by Paul Duff, "'The Synagogue of Satan': Crisis Mongering and the *Apocalypse of John*," which the author kindly allowed me to read before its publication; now published in *The Reality of Apocalypse: Rhetoric and Politics in the Book of Revelation* (Atlanta: Society of Bibilical Literature, 2006). See also Steven Friesen, "Sarcasm in Revelation 2–3: Churches, Christians, True Jews, and Satanic Synagogues," in David Barr, ed., *The Reality of Apocalypse: Rhetoric and Politics in the Book of Revelation* (Atlanta: Society of Biblical Literature, 2006), 127–144.

75 Duff, *Who Rides the Beast?* 53.

76 Aune, *Revelation 1–5*, vol. 52A, cxxi. For the more traditional view that John here denounces actual Jews, see, for example, Yarbro Collins, "Conflict with Jews," wherein she states that in John's letters, "the name 'Jews' is denied to the Jewish community in Smyrna . . . because the followers of Jesus are held to be the true Jews," in *Crisis and Catharsis*, 85ff. Prigent agrees that, for John, "the Jews . . . are truly a synagogue of Satan . . . who denounce Christians," 78–79. Throughout his well-informed and influential commentary, Prigent confidently asserts that when John speaks of Israel, he actually means "Christians": "In the eyes of the seer, *for whom the people of God is made up of*

Christians, these Jews have obviously ceased deserving to belong to Israel," *Commentary*, 152. Prigent later declares that "for our author, the true Israel, *the only true people of God, are the Christians*." *Commentary*, 284. (All italics mine.)

77 On the term *Christianoi*, see Philippa Townsend, "Who Were the First Christians? Jews, Gentile, and the *Christianoi*," in Eduard Iricinschi and Holger M. Zellentin, eds., *Heresy and Identity in Late Antiquity* (Tübingen, Germany: Mohr Siebeck, 2008), 212–230.

78 Pliny to Trajan, Letter X, 96.3; Trajan's reply, Letter X, 97 1–2.

79 Acts 11:26.

80 The church leader Irenaeus, himself a Gentile convert who came from his native city of Smyrna to Gaul, traces the teaching of another group of believers whom John of Patmos despises and calls Nicolitains to a man named Nicolaus, whom the Book of Acts identifies as "a proselyte from Antioch" (Acts 6:5), apparently another Syrian converted to what Paul had preached. As we shall see, it is Ignatius, also a Syrian convert to Paul's teaching, who is the first, so far as we know, to insist on being called a Christian.

81 Acts 15:20.

82 Romans 11:17–24.

83 Romans 11:18–20; 3:27. See the corrective work of John Gager, who rightly identifies Paul as a first-century Jew, in his book *Reinventing Paul* (Oxford, UK: Oxford University Press, 2000).

84 Romans 2:28–29.

85 Romans 9:2–3, to mention only one example. For more citations and an incisive discussion, see Daniel Boyarin, *Carnal Israel: Reading Sex in Talmudic Culture* (Berkeley: University of California Press, 1993).

86 Romans 9:8.

87 Galatians 3:7, 23–29, 4:21–31.

88 Galatians 6:16.

89 Revelation 3:9.

90 Hans Conzelmann, "Paulus und die Weisheit," in *New Testament Studies* 12: 231–244; Meeks, *The First Urban Christians*, 40–50.

91 We do not know the date of Ignatius' conversion; he may, in fact, have grown up in a Christian family. Historians place his birth date around 50 C.E. and the date of his death between 98 and 117 C.E. For a detailed and careful analysis of the evidence, see Christine Trevett, *A Study of Ignatius of Antioch in Syria and Asia* (Lewiston, NY: Edwin Mellen Press, 1992).

92 Ignatius, Letter to the Romans, IV.

93 The date is debatable, with guesses ranging from 98 to 117. For discussion, see Trevett, *A Study of Ignatius.*

94 I Corinthians 12:28.

95 See Akira Satake, *Die Gemeindeordnung in der Johannesapokalypse* (Neukirchen-Vluyn, Germany: Neukirchen, 1966); see also Hans-Josef Klauck, who states that John's silence about priests and bishops "must be deliberate and intensely polemical," in his article "Das Sendschreiben nach Pergamon und der Kaiserkult," *Biblica* 73 (1992): 153–182; and Pagels, "The Social History of Satan, Part III," 501–505.

96 Ignatius, Letter to the Trallians, 3.1–3.

97 Revelation 21:14. John says he sees their names inscribed on the twelve foundations of the wall surrounding the New Jerusalem, suggesting that he sees them as founders of the future kingdom.

98 Revelation 2:2.

99 See discussion by Trevett in *A Study of Ignatius,* and also the articles cited in the following note.

100 See Christine Trevett, *Montanism: Gender, Authority, and the New Prophecy* (Cambridge, UK: Cambridge University Press, 2002), 23, 142–144; "Prophecy and Anti-Episcopal Activity: A Third Error Combated by Ignatius?" *Journal of Ecclesiastical*

History (1983): 1–18; "Apocalypse, Ignatius, Montanism: Seeking the Seeds," *Vigiliae Christianae* 43 (1989): 313–338.

101 Ignatius, Letter to the Philadelphians, 7.1–2.

102 Mark 1:2–3.

103 I owe the metaphor to Prigent, *L'Apocalypse de Saint Jean* (Geneva: Labor et Fides, 1988), 41.

104 Trevett notes in Ignatius' letters three allusions to passages in the Hebrew Bible, while Ignatius refers to Paul's writings dozens of times.

105 Ignatius, Letter to the Philadelphians, 8.1–2.

106 Perhaps the earliest reference to Paul's letters as part of "the Scriptures" occurs in 2 Peter 3:15–16, probably written in the early or mid–second century. Codices containing Paul's collected letters began to be circulated in some groups as early as the second to third centuries; the earliest lists that include them as part of a "canonical" collection date to the fourth century, from Eusebius' *History of the Church*, and canon lists from the time of Cyril of Jerusalem; for discussion, see chapter 5.

107 Ignatius, Letter to the Philadelphians; Letter to the Magnesians, 10.3.

108 Ignatius, Letter to the Magnesians, 10.1.

109 For an incisive and influential discussion of the term as second-century authors used it, see Denise Buell, *Why This New Race? Ethnic Reasoning in Early Christianity* (New York: Columbia University Press, 2005).

110 Romans 11.1; 2 Corinthians 11:22.

CHAPTER THREE: Other Revelations: Heresy or Illumination?

Please note: Scholars and students are advised to consult the more complete and technical discussion of the material contained in this chapter, previously published as "Anthony's Letters and

Nag Hammadi Codex 1: Sources of Religious Conflict in Fourth Century Egypt," by Lance Jenott and Elaine Pagels, in the *Journal of Early Christians Studies* 18:4 (2010): 557–589.

1 Norman R. Cohn, *The Pursuit of the Millennium: Revolutionary Millenarians and Mystical Anarchists of the Middle Ages* (New York: Oxford University Press, 1970).

2 Viktor E. Frankl, *Man's Search for Meaning*, trans. Ilse Lasch (Boston: Beacon Press, 2006), 40–41, 69.

3 Wolfson, *Through a Speculum That Shines: Vision and Imagination in Medieval Jewish Mysticism* (Princeton, NJ: Princeton University Press, 1994), 29. Note that I am not speaking here of a specific genre of literature, notoriously hard to classify, since scholars often take John's Book of Revelation as the paradigm of what they define as a "revelation" text—even though it differs from most others in basic ways (it is not, for example, pseudonymously written). For the former discussion, see the influential study by John J. Collins, *The Apocalyptic Imagination: An Introduction to Jewish Apocalyptic Literature*, and the publications of David Hellholm. Note also how David Frankfurter cites Elisabeth Schüssler Fiorenza: "The very word *apocalypsis* in the earliest Christian texts 'denotes a visionary ecstatic experience similar to prophecy' rather than a literary presentation of esoteric knowledge," in "The Legacy of Jewish Apocalypses in Early Christianity: Regional Trajectories," in William Adler and James C. Vanderkam, eds., *The Jewish Apocalyptic Heritage in Early Christianity* (Assen, Netherlands: Van Gorcum, 1996), 135, and his note on terminology on 156; see also Schüssler Fiorenza's "*Apocalypsis* and *Propheteia*: Revelation in the Context of Early Christian Prophecy," republished in her book *The Book of Revelation* (Minneapolis: Augsburg Fortress, 1998), 133–156.

4 Zostrianos 3.23–31, NHC VIII, 1, in *The Coptic Gnostic Library*, ed. J.A. Robinson (Leiden, Netherlands: Brill, 2000; hereafter cited as *CGL*), vol. 4, 36–37.

5 Zostrianos 5.11–13, *NHC VIII, 1*, in *CGL* vol. 4, 39.

6 The Revelation [Apocalypse] of Peter, 72. 5–9, 15–28, *NHC VII, 3*, in *CGL* vol. 4, 222–225.

7 See Bentley Layton's intriguing article "The Riddle of the Thunder (CG VI,2): The Function of Paradox in a Gnostic Text from Nag Hammadi," in Charles Hedrick and Robert Hodgeson Jr., eds., *Nag Hammadi, Gnosticism, and Early Christianity* (Peabody, MA: Hendrickson, 1986), and Anne McGuire, *Valentinus and the Gnostike Hairesis: An Investigation of Valentinus' Position in the History of Gnosticism,* unpublished dissertation, Yale University, 1983.

8 The Revelation of Ezra, 3.1–3; the citations here, with minor alterations, follow the excellent translation, edition, and commentary by Michael E. Stone, *Fourth Ezra: A Commentary on the Book of Fourth Ezra* (Minneapolis: Fortress Press, 1990).

9 I am grateful to Professor Martha Himmelfarb for noting Salathiel's meaning as a pen name.

10 The Revelation of Ezra, 3.27–32.

11 The Revelation of Ezra, 4.1–5.

12 Job 38:4–7, 19–37.

13 Job 42:1–6.

14 The Revelation of Ezra, 4.12.

15 The Revelation of Ezra, 4.22–24.

16 The Revelation of Ezra, 4.26–6.25.

17 The Revelation of Ezra, 7.29. For discussion, see Stone, *Fourth Ezra*, 208–209, 368–69.

18 The Revelation of Ezra, 4.52.

19 The Revelation of Ezra, 7.75–91.

20 The Revelation of Ezra, 5.15–15.

21 The Revelation of Ezra, 5.34ff.

22 The Revelation of Ezra, 9.24–25. See the incisive discussion by Martha Himmelfarb, *Ascent to Heaven in Jewish and Christian Apocalypses* (Oxford, UK: Oxford University Press, 1993),

especially 98–100, 106–107; *The Apocalypse: A Brief History* (Chichester, UK: Wiley-Blackwell, 2010), 55–62, as well as Stone's edition and commentary cited above.

23 The Revelation of Ezra, 9.38–10.16.

24 For an outstanding review of scholarly discussion of the composition of the text, as well as a fascinating analysis of how the text describes Ezra's "change of heart," see Stone, *Fourth Ezra*, especially 11–47, 302–331.

25 The Revelation of Ezra, 10.26–54. See also Stone's discussion and comparison with John of Patmos' account of the holy city of Jerusalem.

26 The Revelation of Ezra, 14:38–41.

27 The Revelation of Ezra, 14:44–47.

28 We can see that this book was widely read by Christians in antiquity; Irenaeus seems to have known the book, or much of its contents. Of the thirteen volumes found at Nag Hammadi, each containing a number of ancient texts, three include copies of the Secret Revelation of John. A fourth copy survives in the so-called Berlin Codex 8502, 2. For discussion of the textual evidence, along with parallel transcription of the texts, with translation and commentary, see Michael Waldstein and Frederik Wisse, *The Apocryphon of John: Synopsis of Nag Hammadi Codices II, 1; III, 1, and IV, 1, with BG 8502, 2* (Leiden, Netherlands: Brill, 1995), 1–8. For a more recent translation, along with scholarly discussion, see Karen L. King, *The Secret Revelation of John* (Cambridge, MA: Harvard University Press, 2006), and for a fascinating discussion of the Secret Revelation in relation to Irenaeus' critique, see her "Social and Theological Effects of Heresiological Discourse," in Eduard Iricinschi and Holger M. Zellentin, eds., *Heresy and Identity in Late Antiquity* (Tübingen, Germany: Mohr Siebeck, 2008), 28–49.

29 The Secret Revelation [Apocryphon] of John, *II.1.3–2.4, NHC II, 1,* in *CGL* vol. 2, 13–19.

30 To see how scholars disagree on the translation of this passage, compare, for example, the translation by Michael Waldstein and Frederick Wisse in *The Coptic Gnostic Library,* vol. 2, 17; Karen L. King, *The Secret Revelation of John,* 27; and Zlatko Plese, *The Apocryphon of John: Narrative, Cosmology, Composition,* Ph.D. dissertation, Yale University, 1996, 28ff.

31 The Secret Revelation of John, *NHC II, 2,* 2–6; 6, 14; see, for example, *CGL* vol. 2, 17–35, 85, 113. Note that the version transmitted in Codex II often uses the term "Mother-Father," while other versions (Codex III and the Berlin Codex, for example) differ. For discussion of gendered language, see King, *Secret Revelation,* 125–136.

32 The Secret Revelation of John, *NHC II, 25,* 1–15, in *CGL* vol. 2, 147.

33 The Secret Revelation of John, *NHC II,* 26.6–7, in *CGL* vol. 2, 151. Note: I have offered here a slightly different translation of the Coptic *rome nim* as "every human being" (instead of "every man").

34 The Secret Revelation of John, *NHC II, 31, 9,* in *CGL* vol. 2, 175. Here, too, I have offered a freer translation of the Coptic phrase that speaks of the "immovable race," in order to convey its meaning, as interpreted by Michael Williams in his influential monograph *The Immovable Race: A Gnostic Designation and the Theme of Stability in Late Antiquity* (Leiden, Netherlands: Brill, 1995).

35 The Secret Revelation of James, *1.9–2.15, NHC I, 1; CGL* vol. 1, 28–31 (here, too, minor alterations in the translation).

36 Acts 1:9–10.

37 The Secret Revelation of James, *2.20–26, NHC I, 1, CGL* vol. 1, 30–31.

38 The Secret Revelation of James, 9.1–9, *NHC I, 1,* in *CGL* vol. 1, 40–43.

39 The Secret Revelation of James, 6.19–20, *NHC I, 1,* in *CGL* vol. 1, 36–37.

40 The Secret Revelation of James, 15.6–29, *NHC I, 1,* in *CGL* vol. 1, 50–53.

41 For a discussion of ascent as exemplified in *NHC XI, 3,* the text called Allogenes, in relation to the pattern of ascent described by Plato and taught by his disciple Plotinus, see Karen L. King, *Revelation of the Unknowable God: With Text, Translation, and Notes to NHC XI, 3 Allogenes* (Santa Rosa, CA: Polebridge Press, 1995: 9–16, and also the brilliant essay by John Turner, which compares philosophical and Jewish practices of ascent, "The Gnostic Threefold Path to Enlightenment: The Ascent of Mind and the Descent of Wisdom," in *Novum Testamentum* 22 (1980), 324–35. For a discussion of Jewish apocalyptic practice in light of psychoanalytic perspectives, see Dan Merkur, "The Visionary Practices of Jewish Apocalyptists," in *Psychoanalytic Study of Society* 14 (1989), 119–148.

42 For an early study of these dialogues, see Pheme Perkins, *The Gnostic Dialogue: The Early Church and the Crisis of Gnosticism* (New York: Paulist Press, 1980).

43 Matthew 18:20.

44 The Prayer of the Apostle Paul, A.1.5–B.29, *NHC I, A–B,* in *CGL* vol. 1, 8–9. The Secret Revelation of James is bound into the same volume, which scholars call Codex I, as the first of five writings. For discussion of this text, see chapter 5, pages 149–153.

45 The Dialogue of the Savior, 135.28–136.3, *NHC III, 5,* in *CGL* vol. 3, 70–71.

46 Irenaeus, *Against Heresies,* I.13.2.

47 Irenaeus, *Against Heresies,* I.20.1. For a discussion of the evidence that Irenaeus read this work or another with similar

content, see Karen L. King, *The Secret Revelation of John*, 17, and especially her article on the topic cited in note 28.

48 The Dialogue of the Savior, 139.53, NHC III, 5, in CGL vol. 3, 78–79.

49 The Gospel of Truth, 17.5–20, NHC I, 3, in CGL vol. 1, 82–83.

50 The Gospel of Truth, 42.11–20, NHC I, 3, in CGL vol. 1, 116–117.

51 The Discourse on the Eighth and Ninth, 52.2–6, NHC VI, 6, in CGL vol. 3, 346–347.

52 The Discourse on the Eighth and Ninth, 52.6–7, NHC VI, 6, in CGL vol. 3, 346–347; 55.4–17, in CGL vol. 3, 352–353.

53 The Discourse on the Eighth and Ninth, 57.30–58.17, NHC VI, 6, in CGL vol. 3, 356–361.

54 The Discourse on the Eighth and Ninth, 59.24–61.15, NHC VI, 6, in CGL vol. 3, 362–367.

55 Allogenes, 52.8–12, NHC XI, 3, in CGL vol. 5, 206–207. For the sake of consistency, I continue to cite the text and translation in Robinson's *The Coptic Gnostic Library*; see also the excellent text and translation, with commentary and introduction, by King, *Revelation of the Unknowable God*.

56 Allogenes, 56.15–20, NHC XI, 3, in CGL vol. 5, 214–215; note that the text is broken here and partially reconstructed, and I have slightly altered the translation.

57 Allogenes, 57.26–31, NHC XI, 3, in CGL vol. 5, 217.

58 Allogenes, 59.26–60.8, NHC XI, 3, in CGL vol. 5, 220–223.

59 Allogenes, 59.36ff., NHC XI, 3, in CGL vol. 5, 222–225.

60 Allogenes, 68.25–31, NHC XI, 3, in CGL vol. 5, 238–239.

61 The Greek term *teleios*, often translated "perfect," connotes what is "full, complete, mature."

62 Gospel of John 12:28–30.

63 Thunder, Perfect Mind, 13.1–14.2, NHC VI, 2, in CGL vol. 3, 234–237; cf. Layton, "The Riddle of the Thunder," and also Anne McGuire's discussion in *Searching the Scriptures, Vol. 2: A*

Feminist Commentary, Elisabeth Schüssler Fiorenza, ed. (New York: Herder & Herder, 1994), 39–54.

64 Thunder, Perfect Mind, 16.6–17.25, NHC VI, 2, in CGL vol. 3, 240–243.

65 Thunder, Perfect Mind, 18.8–19.33, NHC VI, 2, in CGL vol. 3, 246–251.

66 Trimorphic Protennoia, 35.11–36.28, NHC XIII, 1, in CGL vol. 5, 402–405.

67 Many commentators have noted that John's apocalypse seems intended for reading or recitation in worship; for discussion, see the fine analysis of Pierre Prigent, *Commentary on the Apocalypse of St. John,* trans. Wendy Pradels (Tübingen, Germany: Mohr Siebeck, 2001). For an incisive and intriguing discussion in English, see David L. Barr, *Tales of the End: A Narrative Commentary on the Book of Revelation* (Santa Rosa, CA: Polebridge Press, 1985).

68 *The Teachings of Silvanus,* 106.30–117.20, NHC VII, 4, in CGL vol. 4, 336–367.

69 The Gospel of Phillip 67:25–26, NHC II, 3, in CGL vol. 2, 176–177.

70 For discussion, see chapter 5, 138ff.

CHAPTER FOUR: Confronting Persecution:
How Jews and Christians Separated Politics from Religion

1 Epiphanius, *Panarion,* 49.1. David Frankfurter, in his article "The Legacy of Jewish Apocalypses," correctly notes that this allusion alone does not establish dependence on John's book (137). However, the evidence for John's influence on the movement includes other data mentioned here, including the controversy over the Gospel of John and the Book of Revelation, which it partly occasioned; see also Christine Trevett's discussion of the topic in *Montanism: Gender, Authority, and the New*

Prophecy (Cambridge, UK: Cambridge University Press, 1996; cited from paperback edition, 2002), 130–139. On the "new Jerusalem," see William Tabbernee, "Portals of the Montanist New Jerusalem: The Discovery of Pepouza and Tymion," *Journal of Early Christian Studies* 11:1, 87–89e. I am grateful to Elizabeth Clark for pointing out this intriguing article.

2 Timothy D. Barnes, *Tertullian: A Historical and Literary Study* (Oxford, UK: Oxford University Press, 1971), 131.

3 Tertullian, *Apology*, 37.

4 See discussion by Meeks, *The First Urban Christians.*

5 Tertullian, *Ad Nationes*, I, 7.

6 Isaiah 65:17–25.

7 Epiphanius, *Panarion*, 49.11.

8 Epiphanius, *Panarion*, 48.4.

9 Revelation 2:4. For a detailed discussion of the movement, see Trevett's *Montanism*, cited in note 1, and also Laura Nasrallah, *"An Ecstasy of Folly": Prophecy and Authority in Early Christianity* (Cambridge, MA: Harvard University Press, 2003).

10 Epiphanius, *Panarion*, 48.12.

11 Eusebius, *History of the Church* (hereafter cited as *HE*, from *Historia Ecclesiae*) Book 5.16.

12 Justin, *Dialogue with Trypho*, 82, 1ff., in *St. Justin Martyr: Dialogue with Trypho*, trans. Thomas B. Falls (Washington, D.C.: Catholic University Press, 2003), 128.

13 Justin, *Dialogue with Trypho*, 81, 4, 127.

14 Justin, *Dialogue with Trypho*, 82, 2, 128.

15 Justin, *Second Apology 1*, in *St Justin Martyr: The First and Second Apologies*, trans. Leslie Barnard (Mahwah, NJ: Paulist Press, 1997), 73. See also discussions mentioned in the following note.

16 Justin, *Apology*, 1. For discussion and citations, see Pagels, "Christian Apologists and the 'Fall of the Angels': An Attack on Roman Imperial Power?" in *Harvard Theological Review* 78

(1985): 301–325. For a more accessible discussion, see Pagels, "Satan's Earthly Kingdom: Christians Against Pagans," in *The Origin of Satan: How Christians Demonized Jews, Pagans, and Heretics* (New York: Vintage, 1995), 112–148.

17 Justin, *Apology*, 45.

18 Justin, *Apology*, 12. For a fine discussion of reactions among the imperial circle, see Victor Schmidt, "Reaktionen auf das Christentum in den *Metamorphosen* des Apuleius," in *Vigiliae Christianae* 51 (1997): 21–71.

19 Justin, *Apology*, 17.

20 E. Mary Smallwood, *The Jews Under Roman Rule from Pompey to Diocletian: A Study in Political Relations* (Leiden, Netherlands: Brill, 1981), 47–149.

21 Josephus, *Antiquities of the Jews* 16, 6, 1–2; see also Glen Bowersock, "C. Marius Censorinus Legatus Caesaris," *Harvard Studies in Classical Philology* 68 (1964): 207.

22 See Smallwood, *The Jews Under Roman Rule*, 115–143; also the comments by Peter Schäfer, *Judeophobia: Attitudes Toward the Jews in the Ancient World* (Cambridge, MA: Harvard University Press, 1997), 136ff; also note the essays published by Judith Lieu, John North, and Tessa Rajak, eds., in *The Jews Among Pagans and Christians in the Roman Empire* (London and New York: Routledge, 1992).

23 Philo, *De Legatione ad Gaium*, 357, in *Philo: Vol. X*, trans. F. H. Colson and J. W. Earp (Bury St. Edmunds, UK: Loeb Classical Library, 1962), 178–179.

24 *The Martyrdom of Justin, Chariton, Charito, Evelpistis, Hierax, Paeon, and Valerian*, 5.6. (hereafter cited as *The Acts of Justin*, from *The Acts of the Christian Martyrs*, trans. Herbert Musurillo (Oxford, UK: Clarendon Press, 1972), 47.

25 *The Letter of the Churches of Lyons and Vienne*, 1.4, in Musurillo, *Acts of the Christian Martyrs*, 62–63.

26 On the image of "the beast" as Rome, menacing the martyrs, see *The Letter of the Churches of Lyons and Vienne*, 1.5, 42, 57, 2.6. Note, too, that an earlier passage (1.10) quotes Revelation 14:4, while 1.57 quotes Revelation 22:1 and refers to John's book among "the scriptures."

27 Irenaeus, *Against Heresies*, III.11.9.

28 Irenaeus, *Against Heresies*, III.3.4.

29 Irenaeus, *Against Heresies*, V.26.1.

30 Irenaeus, *Against Heresies*, V.25.1ff. For one early interpretation of the Antichrist traditions, see Wilhelm Bousset, *The Antichrist Legend: A Chapter in Christian and Jewish Folklore*, trans. A. H. Keane (Atlanta: Scholars Press, 1999), with an updated introduction by David Frankfurter.

31 I John 4:3.

32 Daniel 7:7ff; Irenaeus, *Against Heresies*, V.25.3.

33 John 5:43; Irenaeus, *Against Heresies*, V.25.4. As noted in note 31, we find in I John 4:3 the prophecy of a deceiver called "antichrist."

34 "Those who believe willingly do God's will, by their own choice; but those who disobey, by their own choice do not accept his doctrine," in *Against Heresies*, V.27.1. Brian E. Daley, in his influential book on early Christian apocalyptic sources, observes that Hippolytus of Rome, who wrote his *Refutation of All Heresies* and his treatise *De Christo et Antichristo* during the early third century, "promises *to the orthodox*... [that] he shall escape 'the threat of fiery judgment,' and 'the ever-threatening eye of Tarturus' punishing angels' (10.24.2) to become 'a familiar companion of God and a fellow-heir of Christ'" (italics mine). See *The Hope of the Early Church: A Handbook of Patristic Eschatology* (Cambridge, UK: Cambridge University Press, 1991), 40.

35 Irenaeus, *Against Heresies*, V.26.2.

36 Irenaeus, *Against Heresies*, V.30.3.

37 Irenaeus, *Against Heresies*, V.30.3.

38 Pliny, *Letter to Trajan*, Letter X.9; see 5–10.

39 Although Fronto's speech is lost, Minuncius Felix gives this account of what he said in *Octavius*, 9.6, and Tertullian may be echoing and satirizing other aspects of that famous speech in *Apology* 2 and 7.

40 *The Martyrdom of Justin*, 5, 1–3, in Musurillo, *Acts of the Martyrs*, 47.

41 Celsus' *True Doctrine* survives only in fragments preserved in a book that the Christian teacher Origen wrote to refute his influential polemic. For a reconstructed translation of Celsus' work, see Celsus, *On the True Doctrine: A Discourse Against the Christians*, with introduction and translation by R. Joseph Hoffmann (Oxford, UK: Oxford University Press, 1987). Origen's book against Celsus is well translated and annotated by Henry Chadwick in his *Origen: Contra Celsum* (Cambridge, UK: Cambridge University Press, 1965). For an excellent discussion of how members of Marcus' circle reacted to the Christian movement, see Victor Schmidt, "Reakionen auf das Christentum in den Metamorphosen des Apuleius," in *Vigiliae Christianae* 51 (Leiden, Netherlands: Brill, 1997), 51–71.

42 This suggestion is made by Schmidt, "Reaktionen auf das Christentum," 61.

43 Origen, *Contra Celsum*, 4.11.

44 Origen, *Contra Celsum*, V.14.

45 Origen, *Contra Celsum*, I.1; see also VIII.17–68.

46 Tertullian, *Against the Jews (Adversus Judaeos)*, 9.15, in G. D. Dunn, *Tertullian*, in the series *The Early Church Fathers* (London: Routledge, 2004), 87.

47 See Timothy D. Barnes, "Pre-Decian *Acta Martyrum*," in *Journal of Theological Studies* 19, n.s. 19 (1968): 433–437.

48 *The Passion of Perpetua and Felicitas*, 18.8, in Musurillo, *Acts of the Christian Martyrs*, 126–127.

49 *The Passion of Perpetua and Felicitas*, 10.1–25, in Musurillo, *Acts of the Christian Martyrs*, 116–119. For discussion of these allusions to Revelation in the account of Perpetua's martyrdom, see R. Petraglio, "Des influences de l'Apocalypse dans la *Passio Perpeutuae* 11–13," in *L'Apocalypse de Jean: Traditions exégétiques et iconographiquest, III–XIII siècles* (Geneva: Librarie Droz, 1979), 15–29; see also David P. Armstrong-Reiner, *"You Opened the Book": An Instrumental Understanding of the Patristic Use of the Revelation of John*, unpublished dissertation, Emory University, May 2008.

50 Tertullian, *De Spectaculis*, 30.

51 Tertullian, *Apology*, 30.

52 Matthew 22:21.

53 Romans 13:1.

54 Tertullian, *Apology*, 32, 39.

55 Tertullian, *Apology*, 39.

56 Apuleius, *Apology*, 55–56.

57 In this respect, other evidence suggests that he was right; note, for example, that these are some of the same charges that Irenaeus threw against Marcus, the visionary teacher active in his district, as well as in Asia Minor, whom he called a fraud and heretic and accused of practicing magic and seducing rich women; see, for example, *Against Heresies* I, 13.1–6.

58 Apuleius, *Apology*, 25–26.

59 Apuleius, *Apology*, 26.

60 Apuleius, *Apology*, 28.

61 Although this is the popular title, Apuleius aptly called it *The Metamorphoses*, since, as we shall see, its primary theme is transformation.

62 Apuleius, *The Golden Ass*, 9, 14.

63 Apuleius, *The Golden Ass*, 11, 16–24; in section 23, Apuleius writes that "the initiation ceremony took the form of a kind of voluntary death, and salvation through divine grace."

64 Justin, *Apology*, 61.

65 Pliny, Letter to Trajan, Letter X, 96.

66 Timothy D. Barnes, *Tertullian*, 258. For an excellent account of how the Christian message traveled, see Meeks, *The First Urban Christians*.

67 Tertullian, *De Testimonio Animae*, 1.

68 Tertullian, *De Testimonio Animae*, 6.

69 Tertullian, *De Testimonio Animae*, 1.

70 Tertullian, *Apology*, 24–25.

71 Tertullian, *Apology*, 12–13.

72 Tertullian, *Apology*, 4.

73 Tertullian, *De Testimonio Animae*, 2.

74 Tertullian, *Apology*, 33–34.

75 Tertullian, *Apology*, 24.

76 Tertullian, *To Scapula*, 2: *Tamen humani iuris et naturalis potestatis est unicuique quod putaverit, colere nec alii obest aut prodest alterius religio.*

77 As is well-known, the writers of this Declaration apparently had in mind only men like themselves—property-owning, Caucasian males—although since their time, of course, most Americans have come to apply it to all people, or at least to all citizens.

CHAPTER FIVE: Constantine's Conversion:
How John's Revelation Became Part of the Bible

1 Eusebius, *HE* 8.5.1; Lactantius, *De Mortibus Persecutorum*, 12, 2–4. Note that there were, as Professor Elizabeth Clark kindly reminded me in a letter, a series of decrees regarding treatment of Christians. These events are also discussed in

Timothy D. Barnes, *Constantine and Eusebius* (Cambridge, MA: Harvard University Press, 1981), 22.

2 On the number, see William Telfer, "St. Peter of Alexander and Arius," *Analecta Bollandiana* 67 (1949): 126; Eusebius, *HE*, 8.6–10.10; Timothy D. Barnes, *Constantine and Eusebius*, 201. On Melitius' refusal, see William Telfer, "Melitius of Lycopolis and Episcopal Succession in Egypt," *Harvard Theological Review* 48.4 (1955): 227–237.

3 Lactantius, *De Mortibus Persecutorum*, 33–34.

4 Eusebius, *HE*, 9.6.2.

5 Eusebius, *Life of Constantine*, Book 1, 28–29, in Eusebius, *Life of Constantine: Introduction, Translation, and Commentary*, eds. and trans. Averil Cameron and Stuart George Hall (New York: Oxford University Press, 1999), 80–81.

6 See Lactantius, *De Mortibus Persecutorum*, 48.2–12, for the entire text of the so-called Edict of Milan, in which Constantine and Licinius declare that "our purpose is to grant both to the Christians and to all others full authority to follow whatever worship each one has desired, so that whatever divinity dwells in heaven may be benevolent and propitious to us, and to all placed under our authority."

7 See, for example, Fergus Millar, "Edicts and *Epistolae*: Toleration, Restitution, and *Beneficia*," in *The Emperor in the Roman World* (Ithaca, NY: Cornell University Press, 1977), 577–584.

8 Ian Boxall has noted Athanasius' interpretative move, and some of its later effects, in his article "The Many Faces of Babylon the Great: *Wirkungsgeschichte* and the Interpretation of Revelation 17," in *Studies in the Book of Revelation*, ed. Steve Moyise (London: T&T Clark, 2000), 51–68.

9 See John Teall, "The Grain Supply of the Byzantine Empire," *Dumbarton Oaks Papers* 13 (1955): 90–96: Michael J. Hollerich, "The Alexandrian Bishops and the Grain Trade: Ecclesiastical

Commerce in Late Roman Egypt," *Journal of the Economic and Social History of the Orient* 25.2 (1982): 187–207.

10 Barnes, *Constantine and Eusebius*, 224.

11 For some discussion, see pages 138–139. On Arius, see Rowan Williams, *Arius*, 2nd ed. (London: SCM Press, 1987), 41–61; Robert Gregg and Dennis Groh, *Early Arianism: A View of Salvation* (Minneapolis: Fortress Press, 1981); Lewis Ayers, *Nicea and Its Legacy: An Approach to Fourth Century Trinitarian Theology* (New York: Oxford University Press, 2005).

12 Eusebius, *Life of Constantine*, Book 2, 63, in Cameron and Hall, 115–116; see also Barnes, *Constantine and Eusebius*, 200–202.

13 Constantine, *Letter to Alexander and Arius*, cited in Eusebius' *Life of Constantine*, Book 2, 64–72; for a clear translation with introduction and commentary, see Eusebius, *Life of Constantine*, translated and with introduction and commentary by Cameron and Hall (Oxford: Clarendon Press, 1999), 116–119.

14 The literature about the Arian controversy is famously voluminous; the books mentioned in note 11, and the bibliographies contained in both, offer a good place to start.

15 The number is disputed, and uncertain; Eustathius of Antioch estimates that there were more than 275; see *Life of Constantine*, Book 3, 6.1; 9, in Cameron and Stuart, 123–124; and Theodoret, *Historia Ecclesiae*, I.7, 32.3; Athanasius, *Apol. Contra Arianos*, I, claims that there were "more than three hundred"; see also *De Decretis* 3 and *Historia Arianorum* 67. In *Ep ad Afros* 2, however, he suggests the symbolically charged number 318. Scholars comparing the accounts have challenged this number; Ernest Honigmann, for example, offers a much reduced estimate in "La liste originale des Pères de Nicée," *Byz* 14 (1939): 17–76; see Williams' discussion in *Arius*, 67; Barnes suggests "nearly three hundred" in the account he offers in *Constantine and Eusebius*, 214.

16 See, for example, his *Letter to the Bishops of Egypt*, 13, and his treatise *On the Synods*.

17 While discussion of the theological implications of the Greek term *homoousios* is beyond the scope of our historical focus here, one can find some useful discussion in Gregg and Groh, *Early Arianism*; Williams, *Arius*, 95–214; Khaled Anatolios, *Athanasius: The Coherence of His Thought* (New York: Routledge, 1998); Lewis Ayres, *Nicea and Its Legacy: An Approach to Fourth Century Trinitarian Theology* (New York: Oxford University Press, 2004); and Thomas G. Weinandy, *Athanasius: A Theological Introduction* (Hampshire, UK: Ashgate Publishing, 2007).

18 Note that Christians like Melitius, who "confessed" before a magistrate and so had risked their lives but had not been killed, were recognized by their fellow Christians not as *martyrs*, but *confessors*.

19 For discussion, see Philostorgius, *Historia Ecclesiae* 2.11, 3.11; Sozomen, *Historia Ecclesiae* 2.17.4; Socrates, *Historia Ecclesiae* 1.23; Athanasius, *Apologia Contra Arianos*, 6.4; Leslie Barnard, *Studies in Athanasius' Apologia Secunda*, European University Studies XXIII, vol. 467 (Bern, Switzerland: Peter Lang, 1992), 38–41; Barnes, *Constantine and Eusebius*, 230.

20 Barnard points out, however, "many examples of fluidity in episcopal appointments" among Athanasius' near contemporaries, including those of Ambrose and Augustine; see *Studies in Athanasius' Apologia Secunda*, in European University Studies XXIII, vol. 467 (Bern, Switzerland: Peter Lang, 1992), 40–41.

21 Places to start investigating how he did this include Susannah Elm's incisive study of Athanasius' effort to supervise women ascetics in *Virgins of God: The Making of Asceticism in Late Antiquity* (New York: Oxford University Press, 1994); and especially the learned and influential contribution by David

Brakke, *Athanasius and Asceticism* (Baltimore: Johns Hopkins University Press, 1995), originally published as *Athanasius and the Politics of Asceticism* (New York: Oxford University Press, 1995). The important book by Annick Martin offers a careful investigation and discussion of the evidence: *Athanase d'Alexandrie et l'Église d'Égypte au IVe siècle (328–373)*, (Rome: École Francaise de Rome, 1996), especially part three, "*Le Champ des Forces dans l'Église D'Égypte a l'Avenement de d'Athanase.*"

22 Wilhelm Bousset, *The Antichrist Legend;* see also Hippolytus' comments on Antichrist in *De Christo et Antichristo* and others who characterized heretics as deceived by Satan, and Armstrong-Reiner's discussion of patristic references to Antichrist, "*You Opened the Book,*" 55–218.

23 "Athanasius *contra mundum,*" as he was frequently called; cited in Weinandy's appreciative introduction to his theology, in *Athanasius*, vii; for the other characterization, see Athanasius' *Apologia Contra Arianos*, 9.

24 Timothy D. Barnes, *Athanasius and Constantius: Theology and Politics in the Constantinian Empire* (Cambridge, MA: Harvard University Press, 1993), 32–33; for a view intended to be more balanced and corrective, see, for example, Duane W. H. Arnold, *The Early Episcopal Career of Athanasius of Alexandria* (Notre Dame, IN: University of Notre Dame Press, 1991), 9–95. See also Richard P. C. Hanson, *The Search for the Christian Doctrine of God: The Arian Controversy, 318–381* (London: T&T Clark, 1988), 39ff. For a broader perspective on social conflict in Alexandria, see Christopher Haas, *Alexandria in Late Antiquity: Topography and Social Conflict* (Baltimore: Johns Hopkins University Press, 1997), especially 173–277.

25 Athanasius, *Apologia Contra Arianos*, 90.

26 Athanasius, *Letter to the Bishops of Egypt*, 5; in 9, he calls them "antichrists."

27 Athanasius, *Letter to the Bishops of Egypt*, 22.

28 Athanasius, *Letter to the Bishops of Egypt*, 23.

29 Athanasius, *Historia Arianorum*, 78.1.

30 Athanasius, *Historia Arianorum*, 73, 78.

31 Athanasius, *Historia Arianorum*, 52; on Athanasius' view of his own struggle, see Weinandy, *Athanasius*, 1–10; for a different view, see Barnes, *Athanasius and Constantine*, 53, 121–135.

32 Athanasius, *Historia Arianorum*: comparing Constantius with Antichrist, 67; as forerunner of Antichrist, 70; his appointed bishop as Antichrist, 75–76; Constantius acts like Antichrist, 77–80.

33 Khaled Anatolios, "The Influence of Irenaeus on Athanasius," in *Studia Patristica* XXXVI (Leuven, Belgium: Peeters, 2001), XIII, 463–476, notes other parallels that demonstrate such influence, although he does not mention this one.

34 Although manuscript evidence indicates that Irenaeus' massive book *Against Heresies* was known in Egypt about ten years after he wrote it, we know little about who would have read, much less heeded, his admonitions. Although apparently his work influenced Athanasius (see Anatolios' article cited in note 17), who else read it would depend not only on the uncertainties of book circulation at the time but also on communication between various groups of Christians, as Elizabeth Clark has shown so brilliantly of a later stage of the Origenist controversy; see her book *The Origenist Controversy: The Cultural Construction of an Early Christian Debate* (Princeton, NJ: Princeton University Press, 1992).

35 For an excellent discussion of the state of this question, see James Goehring, "The Provenance of the Nag Hammadi Codices Once More," in *Studia Patristica* 35 (2001): 234–253.

36 For discussion, see the outstanding monograph by Brakke, *Athanasius and Asceticism*.

37 For a good recent overview, see William Harmless, *Desert Chris-*
tians: An Introduction to the Literature of Early Monasticism (New
York: Oxford University Press, 2004). For this period, basic
sources include Athanasius' *Life of Anthony*, discussed below; also
the *Apophthegmata Patrum* ("Sayings of the Fathers"), the *History*
of the Monks in Egypt, and Palladius' *Lausiac History*, as well as
the *Lives of Pachomius*. Significant recent works in English include
Brakke, *Athanasius and Asceticism*; Peter Brown, *The Body and*
Society; Clark, *The Origenist Controversy*; Elm, *Virgins of God*;
James Goehring, *Ascetics, Society, and the Desert* (Harrisburg, PA:
Trinity Press, 1999); and Philip Rousseau, *Ascetics, Authority,*
and the Church (New York: Oxford University Press, 1978).

38 Verba Seniorum XII, 8, cited in Helen Waddell, *The Desert*
Fathers (New York: Vintage, 1998), 117.

39 This brief sketch relies primarily on the clear and incisive
account given by Philip Rousseau in *Pachomius: The Making of a*
Community in Fourth Century Egypt (Berkeley: University of
California Press, 1985).

40 For discussion, see Goehring, "The Provenance of the Nag
Hammadi Codices Once More," cited in note 35 above.

41 Athanasius, *Festal Letter* 39, warns that some Christians, apparently including monks, whom he calls heretics, "were boasting
about the books that they call 'apocryphal,' " and, to his dismay,
"mix these with the divinely inspired Scriptures," use them in
teaching, and refer to them in discussion. See the comments
preceding notes to chapter 3 for reference to the fuller and more
technical version of matters discussed in the rest of this chapter.

42 The Prayer of the Apostle Paul, *NHC I, 1*, in *CGL* vol. 1, 9.

43 I Corinthians 2:10.

44 The Secret Revelation (Apocryphon) of James, in *NHC I, 2*,
in *CGL* vol. 1, 28–29, I, lines 10–19. Recently, scholars of
classical texts have been discussing how readers might have

"experienced" reading or hearing such a codex; see Stephen Emmel, "Religious Tradition, Textual Transmission, and the Nag Hammadi Codices," in *The Nag Hammadi Library After Fifty Years*, ed. John D. Turner and Anne McGuire (Leiden, Netherlands: Brill, 1977), 34–43, and William A. Johnson, "Toward a Sociology of Reading in Classical Antiquity," *American Journal of Philology* 121 (2000): 593–627; for other references, see Jenott and Pagels, "Anthony's Letters and Nag Hammadi Codex I," *Journal of Early Christian Studies* 18.4, 562ff.

45 These two lines are quoted from, respectively, the Secret Revelation of John, NHL II, 1, in CGL vol. 2: I, 18; BG 21.1, 18–19; and the Secret Revelation of James, NHC I, 2, in CGL vol. 1, 31, line 25.

46 While examining the arrangement of texts in the volumes found at Nag Hammadi, a kind of study initiated by Michael Williams in ". . . And What They Left Behind," chapter 11 of *Rethinking "Gnosticism": An Argument for Dismantling a Dubious Category* (Princeton, NJ: Princeton University Press, 1996), 235–262, I realized that many of them, including Codex I and Codex II, open with a scene apparently intended to confound the belief that direct contact with Jesus happened only in the past and to invite the hearer to engage in such contact in the present. For discussion, see Jenott and Pagels, "Anthony's Letters," 558–575.

47 The Secret Revelation of James, NHL I, 2, 3, 11; 6, 20, in CGL vol. 1, 33–37.

48 The Gospel of Truth, in NHL I, 3; 17, 5–24, 9, in CGL vol. 1, 82–93, 117; also 18, 30–11, CGL vol. 1, 84–85

49 See, for example, Paul's first Letter to the Corinthians 15:3, and the Gospel of John 1:29.

50 This point is also noted by David Brakke in his intriguing recent book *The Gnostics: Myth, Ritual, and Diversity in Early Christianity*

(Cambridge, MA: Harvard University Press, 2010), 102. See, too, Harry Attridge's article on Sethian and Valentinian apocalypses, "Valentinian and Sethian Apocalyptic Traditions," in *Journal of Early Christian Studies*, vol. 8, 2 (Summer 2000): 173–211.

51 The Gospel of Truth, *NHL I, 3*; 18, 30–32, CGL vol. 1, 84–85.

52 The Gospel of Truth, *NHL I, 3*; 43, 23–25, in CGL vol. 1, 116–117.

53 Treatise on the Resurrection, *NHL I, 4*, in CGL vol. 1, 148–149, 44, lines 11–12.

54 For example, Matthew 28:9; Luke 24:36–43; John 20:26–29. As Charles H. Dodds has shown, however, the gospel writers juxtapose with such accounts others that suggest that Jesus appeared in *visions*. For reference to his seminal article, and for a fuller discussion, see Pagels, "Visions, Appearances, and Apostolic Authority: Gnostic and Orthodox Traditions," in *Gnosis: Festscrift für Hans Jonas*, ed. Barbara Aland (Göttingen, Germany: Vandenhoek and Ruprecht,1978), 415–430.

55 Acts 10:40–41.

56 I Corinthians 15:50.

57 Treatise on the Resurrection, *NHL I, 4*, in CGL vol. 1, 154–155; 49, lines 21–24.

58 Treatise on the Resurrection, *NHL I, 4*, in CGL vol. 1, 154–155; 48, lines 32–36, 50–151.

59 See the Prayer of Thanksgiving, in *NHL VI, 7*, in CGL vol. 3, 378–387, which apparently includes a scribe's additional note that, after praying in unison, those gathered for worship "embraced each other and went to eat their holy food, which has no blood in it" (apparently, a "pure" vegetarian meal that includes no meat). In the discussion above, I have inferred that the change of tense in the note may suggest that those reading the Discourse, followed by the prayer, in devotions, may have then proceeded to share a "holy meal." For this prayer, placed as it is after the Discourse on the Eighth and Ninth, is known from other

sources, as Jean P. Mahé has pointed out in *Hermès en Haute Égypte. Tome I: Les Textes hermétiques de Nag Hammadi et leurs parallèles grecs et latins*, Bibliotheque Copte de Nag Hammadi, Section "Textes," 3 (Québec: Les Presses de l'Université Laval, 1978) 11–15. See also the discussion by Michael Williams and Lance Jenott, "Inside the Covers of Codex VI," in *Coptica— Gnostica—Manichaica: Mélanges offerts a Wolf-Peter Funk*, ed. Louis Painchaud and Paul H. Poirier (Québec: Les Presses de l'Université Laval, 2006), 1039–1043.

60 Tripartite Tractate, *NHL I, 5*, in *CGL* vol. 1, 192–337, 62, lines 7–10.

61 Tripartite Tractate, *NHL I, 5*, in *CGL* vol. 1, 336–337, 138, lines 22–26.

62 For discussion of a wide range of ancient sources, see Pierre Hadot, *Philosophy as a Way of Life*, cited here from the English translation by Michael Chase (Oxford, UK: Blackwell, 1995).

63 For an excellent review of the long scholarly debate and discussion on this topic, see Goerhing, "The Provenance of the Nag Hammadi Codices Once More."

64 Letters long attributed to Anthony often had been disregarded as pseudonymous, since their content conflicts with much that is found in Athanasius' classic *Life of Anthony*. Like many others, however, I am persuaded by the analysis offered in Samuel Rubenson's book *The Letters of St. Anthony: Monasticism and the Making of a Saint* (Minneapolis: Fortress Press, 1995), that the letters he identifies there are most likely to be genuine.

65 See Thomas Merton, *The Wisdom of the Desert* (New York: New Directions, 1970), 5: "What the Fathers sought most of all, is their own true self, in Christ."

66 *The Letters of St. Anthony*, Letter 6, 84, 222.

67 *The Letters of St. Anthony*, Letter 7, 12, 226; see also Letter 6, 45, 219.

68 *The Letters of St Anthony*, Letter 3, 40, 208.

69 *The Letters of St. Anthony*, Letter 6, 63–71, 220–221.

70 *The Letters of St. Anthony*, 63.

71 *The Letters of St. Anthony*, 64.

72 Peter Brown, *The Body and Society: Men, Women, and Sexual Renunciation in Early Christianity* (New York: Columbia University Press, 1988), adopts this injunction from Origen as the title of his brilliant discussion of Origen's theology, "'I beseech you: Be transformed': Origen," 160–177.

73 James Goehring has carefully investigated the sources to evaluate the number of these monasteries; for his review of the evidence, see his article "The Ship of the Pachomian Federation: Metaphor and Meaning in a Late Account of Pachomian Monasticism," forthcoming in the *Festschrift for Tito Orlandi*. I very much appreciate his expert help in sorting out this question.

74 See, for example, James Goehring, "Monastic Diversity and Ideological Boundaries in Fourth-Century Egypt," in *Ascetics, Society, and the Desert*, 196–220. Notable, too, is the influential study by Elizabeth Clark, *The Origenist Controversy*, which offers a careful and fascinating study of this controversy and concludes by observing that by the early fifth century, "in the West particularly, the broad cosmic vision that had pervaded Origen's theology had shrunk: Christianity now clung more snugly to assertions of human sinfulness, ecclesiastical unity, and obedience to episcopal authority. This more rigid doctrinal dogmatism, coupled with a retreat from issues from cosmology and theodicy, created the religious grounding for the opposition to Origenism," 245–246.

75 For primary sources and incisive discussion, see David Brakke, *Athanasius and Asceticism*, 116–120; also discussion in Jenott and Pagels, "Sources of Religious Conflict," 568ff.

76 Brakke, *Athanasius and Asceticism*, 139.

77 Brakke, *Athanasius and Asceticism*, 115.

78 Many scholars have discussed this issue, notably Robert Gregg and Dennis Groh, "Claims on the Life of St. Anthony," in *Early Arianism*, 131–160, and David Brakke, "The Spirituality and Politics of the Life of Anthony," in *Athanasius and Asceticism*, 201–265, especially 245ff.

79 Athanasius, *Life of Anthony*, 69: "He publically denounced the Arians, declaring that this was the last heresy, the forerunner of Antichrist."

80 The various accounts of Pachomius' life, written in both Coptic and Greek, date from the time after his death, and differ in many details. For discussion, see Rousseau, *Pachomius*, "The Sources," 37–56.

81 Brakke, *Athanasius and Asceticism*, 138–139.

82 Athanasius, *Festal Letter*, 39. David Frankfurter, in his article "The Legacy of Jewish Apocalypses," notes that besides saying that "heretics" value such secret writings, he mentions that some heretics, "particularly the wretched Melitians," boasted of having such books, and so suggests that these may have been Jewish apocalypses that appealed to monks who valued martyrdom, as followers of Melitius did (171). His argument persuasively suggests that the writings Athanasius denounced included such texts. Even if Athanasius were using his polemical words more precisely here than he often did, the evidence of the writings buried near Nag Hammadi suggests, of course, that the banned writings also included other kinds of apocrypha as well.

83 Deuteronomy 4:2; 12:28–32; Revelation 22:18–19; Athanasius, *Festal Letter*, 39, apparently referring to his "list of the books of the New Testament," alludes to Deuteronomy 12:32 when he declares, "Let no one add to or subtract from them."

84 Revelation 22:18–19.

85 For references and discussion of fourth-century discussion on the canon, see Bruce Metzger, *The Canon of the New Testament: Its Origin, Development, and Significance* (Oxford, UK: Clarendon Press, 1987), 209–247.

86 Eusebius, *HE*, 3, 25.1–3.

87 Eusebius, *HE*, 25.4–5.

88 Eusebius, *HE*, 7, 1.

89 For Dionysius' discussion, see Eusebius, *HE*, 7, 24.1–25.27.

90 Revelation 22:18–19.

91 Athanasius, *Letter to the Bishops of Egypt*, 22. I am grateful to David Brakke for pointing out that here Athanasius could have seen himself as following precedent set by Dionysius.

92 Revelation 20:11–21:4.

93 Athanasius, *Defense of Dionysius*, 27.

94 Revelation 20:10.

95 Athanasius, *Festal Letter*, 39.

96 I am grateful to David Brakke for his helpful comments in his letter of March 14, 2011, in which he reminded me of this passage in *Festal Letter*, 39.

97 Eusebius, *Life of Constantine*, Book 3, 3, in Cameron and Hall, 122.

98 Eusebius, *Life of Constantine*, Book 2, 46, in Cameron and Hall, 115.

99 Eusebius, *Life of Constantine*, Book 1, 45, in Cameron and Hall, 88.

100 Eusebius, *Life of Constantine*, Book 2, 62, in Cameron and Hall, 115.

101 Eusebius, *Life of Constantine*, Book 3, 12, 2, in Cameron and Hall, 116.

102 Eusebius, *Life of Constantine*, Book 4, 27, 1, in Cameron and Hall, 163.

CONCLUSION

1 Revelation 20:21.

2 Matthew 25:35–36.

3 Revelation 21:8.

4 For an incisive and learned discussion, see David Frankfurter, *Elijah in Upper Egypt: The Apocalypse of Elijah ad Early Egyptian Christianity* (Minneapolis: Fortress Press, 1993).

5 See Kirsti Barrett Copeland, *Mapping the Apocalypse of Paul: Geography, Genre, and History*, unpublished dissertation, June 2001, Princeton University.

6 The actual quotation is from Theodore Parker, cited by K. Boyle, in *Arc of Justice: A Saga of Race, Civil Rights, and Murder in the Jazz Age* (New York: Henry Holt, 2004).

7 Athanasius, Canons of Athanasius 8

8 Paul, I Corinthians 13:12.

9 Tertullian, *Prescription Against Heresies*, 1–10.

ACKNOWLEDGMENTS

Many friends and colleagues have contributed to the process of completing this book during eight years of research and writing; and since writing is often a solitary process, it's most enjoyable when shared with colleagues, friends, and family. First of all, thanks to Henry Finder, who suggested writing about the Book of Revelation at a time when it sounded like an impossible—or, at least, unlikely—project. After I began thinking about the questions involved, I was especially fortunate that Eric Wanner, director of the Russell Sage Foundation, offered a year's research support among a wonderfully collegial group of colleagues in the social sciences, where conversations over lunch and seminars helped this project take shape. That spring, Tom—director of the Getty Research Institute—and Jack Miles invited me to visit the Institute, which offered glorious views of sky and sun, to be among colleagues conversant with classics, art, and history, who opened up unexpected visions of the Book of Revelation in art and music.

Throughout the years involved in research and writing, as well as teaching, I have enormously appreciated the generosity and learning of colleagues at Princeton University—first of all, those in our working group, John Gager, Martha Himmelfarb, AnneMarie Luijendijk, Napthali Meshel, and Peter Schaefer, each of whom has heard or read drafts of this work in progress, offering helpful criticism and suggestions. I am grateful to Dean David Dobkin and to Carol Rigolot, director of the Humanities Center, and to Susan Stewart, Gideon Rosen, and Alexander Nehemas, and other Princeton colleagues involved in the Humanities Program, for the invaluable support during the final year of writing as Old Dominion Professor at Princeton University. I owe special thanks to Randall Balmer, David Brakke, Tony Campolo, James Cone, Elizabeth Clark, Adela Yarbro Collins, Paul Duff, Elizabeth Fiorenza, Steven Friesen, James Goering, Paul Jeanes, Lance Jenott, Karen King, Jake Mascotte, C. K. Williams, and Michael Williams, each of whom read sections of the manuscript, and offered suggestions that much improved—and often corrected—earlier drafts.

Many thanks to Gabriel Motzin for his generous hospitality as director of the Van Leer Foundation in Jerusalem, and to Israel Yuval, Galit Haken Rosen, and other colleagues at the Hebrew University for kindly inviting me to participate in a seminar and to join a marvelous trip to the Galilee in spring to visit archeological sites. To Eduard Irischinchi I owe thanks for inviting me to join the conference he organized at the Van Leer Foundation, and for the pleasure of his company as we walked from the Dome of the Rock and the rooftop rooms in the Church of the Holy Sepulcher to the walls surrounding the Second Temple, as we traversed places in the Old City we might not have seen without his enthusiastic and expert guidance.

Thanks, too, to the friends and colleagues who invited me to share this work in progress, especially Joan Brown Campbell, Director of Religion at the Chautauqua Institute, and Chautauqua's president, Tom Becker, for their generous hospitality during those lovely summer days. Summers in the Colorado mountains offered a glorious place to write, where I appreciated the invitation Steven Wickes extended to speak about work in progress at the Aspen Institute. I am grateful to the director, Walter Isaacson, himself an amazing writer, and to Amy Margerum; and as every writer will understand, I am enormously grateful to Van Etheridge and Devlen Watkins of the Institute, who, after large sections of the manuscript suddenly disappeared into a black hole on my computer, miraculously recovered them!

As the book began to reach completion, I was especially fortunate to work with Jason Epstein and Wendy Wolf, who smoothed out rough edges and enormously improved the writing. Ever since we first began to work together, Jason has taught me a great deal about writing clearly, and he has become a wonderful friend. Since I came to Viking Press, I've been delighted to work with Wendy, who always found the right questions to ask, and responded with wit, patience, and insight as the project took shape. I owe many thanks to Maggie Riggs and Veronica Windholz for their skillful and meticulous research in the process of copyediting, and to Ben Petrone for his indispensable work and good humor during the process of publication. I am grateful, as always, to longtime friends John Brockman and Katinka Matson, who have always offered excellent advice about publishing—and who, joined by Stewart Brand and Jaron Lanier, engaged in a strategic intervention to save me from a few sentences that struck the wrong note; I finally came to see that they were right!

Meanwhile, at Princeton, Nicole Kirk, now completing her doctoral dissertation, has offered continual—and invaluable—assistance in many ways; and many thanks to Mary Kay Bodnar, Kerry Smith, Patty Bogdziewicz, and Lorraine Fuhrmann, not only for all they do but for the generosity of spirit with which they infuse our department. Finally, the most personal thanks to family members: to my daughter, Sarah, and son-in-law, John DiMatteo, and their beautiful babies, Thomas and Rebekah, to my son, David, and to dear friends for their loving support and for all we share.

INDEX